Down & Dirty Birding

From the Sublime to the Ridiculous—
Here's All the Outrageous but True Stuff
You've Ever Wanted to Know About
North American Birds

Joey Slinger

A FIRESIDE BOOK
PUBLISHED BY SIMON & SCHUSTER

FIRESIDE
Rockefeller Center
1230 Avenue of the Americas
New York, NY 10020

FIRESIDE and colophon are registered trademarks
of Simon & Schuster Inc.

Designed by Chris Welch
Illustrations by Jimmy Holder

Manufactured in the United States of America

1   3   5   7   9   10   8   6   4   2

Library of Congress Cataloging-in-Publication Data

Slinger, Joey.
    Down & dirty birding: from the sublime to the ridiculous—here's
all the outrageous but true stuff you've ever wanted to know about
North American birds / Joey Slinger.
        p.   cm.
    Includes bibliographical references and index.
    1. Birds—Humor.   2. Bird watching—Humor.   3. Birds.   4. Bird
watching.   I. Title.
PN6231.B46S55   1996
598'.072347—dc20   96-315
    ISBN 0-684-80459-X

For Honora

Contents

Introduction

Some years ago, I began my in-depth study of birds, using a text that began, "Examine the skin of a plucked bird—a domestic Fowl or Turkey ready for the oven. Note the pits, or follicles . . ." and thought, There *has* to be some better way.

I looked everywhere, but couldn't find one. That's why I finally decided to create one myself, and now here it is. It is this sort of thing that has made me a recognized authority in the field, if not on pits, or follicles, and without getting too tight-assed about exactly what my authority is recognized for. In any case, no one can deny that this book is packed with information, much of it accurate.

Bird-watching is not for the squeamish or faint of spirit. For years, it was thought to be, and this was the misfortune of many would-be bird-watchers.

What they needed was this book. The first honest look at bird-watchers and the birds they watch. *Down & Dirty Birding* rips away the curtain of lily-white myth that has draped the subject since the Victorian Age and reveals the real myths skulking in the shadows, the suspicions, the hairy-legged half-truths, the envy, the bitter ambition, the treachery. It is not a pretty sight. And they call it a pastime! Life is a pastime; bird-watching is hand-to-hand combat with Mother Nature.

The big trouble with bird-watching is that everybody who approaches it for the first time, or even thinks about approaching it, feels deeply self-conscious and ridiculous. It does no good to point out that there are people who think bird-watching is better than sex. Take a look at them and you can understand why.

What Does Everybody Want to Know?

Everybody wants to know how birds, you know, do it.

It's all here. This *is* the *Down & Dirty Birding* guide, and it offers a great deal more than graphic details of intimate avian moments.

It will also tell you how to get started in bird-watching.

And for those of you who don't need your heads examined, it tells you how to *keep* from getting started in bird-watching.

Down & Dirty Birding Reveals:

🐦 How to become a bird-watching expert without ever leaving the house.

🐦 How to look like an expert.

🐦 How to talk like an expert.

🐦 How to shuck and jive your way through just about anything.

🐦 How to recognize real experts and avoid them.

🐦 And, when you're ready, how to exploit real experts and fake them out of their jocks.

🐦 What's the very best equipment.

🐦 What to wear.

🐦 Where to go.

🐦 How to steer clear of people who think bird-watching is better than sex.

🐦 And what important lessons bird-watching can teach us about life. How to cheat and lie, for example.

Because that's the really nice thing about bird-watching: everybody's opinion is about as good as everybody else's. The drawback is there is no shortage of opinions, and no shortage of individuals prepared to express them.

Part 1

Birders

An A-B-C guide 🐾 *Recognizing bird-watchers in the field* 🐾 *Gear, garb, and inside dope: What it takes to become a birder* 🐾 *How to tell if you have (easy tests you can perform in the privacy of your own home)* 🐾 *And what you can do about it*

Binoculars and Scopes

*Y*ou need binoculars.

It isn't simply that binoculars give you a bigger bird to look at. It's that parts of the bird (some of which are known as "field marks" and are mysteries that will be revealed; some of which are known as "bird parts") are all but impossible to see without binoculars unless you are holding the stupid bird by the neck. For instance, the meadowlark wears a striking yellow sweater (sleeveless) with a black V-neck that you can't see in the normal course of a human-meadowlark intercourse (it perched on a pole, or a wire, or a fence post across a field; you stumbling around in a ditch) without binoculars.

If you have never much used binoculars, you will see screw-all with them at first, anyway. But with hours of practice, dedication, patience, and the sympathetic understanding of loved ones, and an IQ at least into double figures, you will get the hang of it. There was a time, although it seemed like you never would, when you learned to put your food in your mouth and not in your ear. Eventually, you will learn to pick out a bird—even part of a bird—with your binoculars. Some of the dippiest people on earth have managed to do it. If they can, you can.

In choosing binoculars, there is a simple rule to guide you: expensive ones are better. It is this way with everything else in life. Why should it be any different here?

Not that you will necessarily *see* anything better with expensive binoculars, but I'll get to that in a minute. First, what is cheap? *Really* cheap binoculars are ones you got in a store that sells jujubes and body decals. Or else you won them in a carnival contest that involved throwing Nerf Balls at lawn dwarves.

What is not *really* cheap? Binoculars are not really cheap when they have a central thingy for focusing with both eyes and a separate thingy for tuning in your left eye (or your right eye; one or the other, if you have a full set), and don't melt like Kleenex in the rain. This is important, since they will be out in the rain a lot. You need a thingy for focusing one (or the other) side of the binoculars separately because both your eyes may not be the same. This is a terribly complicated procedure and drives a lot of newcomers to throw their binoculars the hell out and take up brain surgery. However, if you persevere, once you get this thingy set, it stays pretty well fixed in place while you spend the rest of your life focusing with the big thingy in the middle.

So two focus thingys. Opera glasses get by with only one because opera glasses are generally under 4-power, and with anything under 4-power, your eyes are pretty evenly balanced, never mind what state the rest of you might be in. There is a new breed of binoculars that doesn't need to be focused, that is always in focus, autofocused or whatever the hell. It's a free country and you can throw your money away on whatever you want, and if you want autofocus binoculars, go ahead and buy them. They don't autofocus on little birdies up as close as the kind you fiddle with yourself, and the image is generally not as sharp.

And now there are binoculars with electronic-focus gizmos like those automatic, idiot-proof cameras. It took real ingenuity to figure out how to add a battery to binoculars, but they've done it. The ads point out that in case the electronic-focus fails, there is a backup manual focus. The ads are telling you more than they think. They are telling you this is a stupid idea.

Binoculars come with numbers on them. For instance, 7×35 is a fairly common number. The first number, in this case the 7, is the amount of magnification—how much bigger a thing will look. The second number, the 35, has to do with how much light the big lenses—the ones at the other end from your eyeballs—let in. To be precise, it is the diameter of the lens in millimeters, but this is what determines the amount of light let in. The more light, the better: 7×50 is better than 7×35, but 7×50 binoculars will pretty much always be a lot bigger than 7×35s and may be too bulky for your tastes, or your physique. Nice is 8×40. Nice magnification, nice amount of light. Usually, you won't need a chiropractor after a day slugging around with them.

You can get some dandy compact little jobs that are 9×25 or the like, some of them even fold up and fit nicely in your pocket or your knapsack. They are very smart-looking, but they are like trying to see what is outside the back door of a giraffe by peering down its throat. Get a pair of real binoculars.

But don't go overboard. You don't want anything stronger than 10×whatever. If somebody sells you something stronger than 10× for bird-watching, it is because they said to themselves, "I will take advantage of this half-wit." Furthermore, you can go to 10×40, maybe, and that is about it. When you get a mittful of 10×50, you will think you are waving a Greyhound bus around. The thing is, 10× is *powerful*. The other thing is, it is probably too powerful, especially if you are an old fart and your hands are not as steady as in the days when you didn't get out of breath climbing out of bed. And especially if you anticipate having a pig-killer of a hangover when you wend toward the wildwood to watch the feathered friends. If your grip trembles, 10× will short out your optic nerves and scramble your brain. (Remember, everything gets magnified, including your tremors.) Another consideration for old farts and the unhawkeyed: If you wear glasses, look for binoculars with rubbery rims around the lenses you press your eyeballs against. Most that are reasonably priced have them. These rims can be folded back to give the bespectacled a bigger picture.

The efficiency of waterproof seals—to keep the insides from fogging up in wet weather—tends to be a function of cost. If you buy expensive glasses, whether they have rubberized "armored" bodies or not, you will spend fewer days with the innards fogged up. If you intend to swim ashore from a submarine before dawn, by all means get the rubberized ones.

But this isn't the reason to buy expensive binoculars. The reason to buy expensive binoculars is that you will see *more* birds with them, particularly if you are a flat-out beginner. You will see more birds because the sight of expensive binoculars impresses the hell out of other bird-watchers. They see these blow-the-kiddies'-college-fund mothers hanging around your neck and naturally assume that you are an expert, because who else in their right mind is going to spend *that kind of money* on binoculars? In instances like this, keep your mouth shut, otherwise you will soon be revealed as a nonexpert, or, in bird-watchers' jargon, a dumb son of a bitch. If you keep your mouth shut, you will be taken for that most admirable of experts, the silent type. So nod a lot and smile a flat kind-of-expert smile. Now, how does this result in your seeing more birds? It results in your seeing more birds because people will *tell* you where the birds are. They will tell you this because there is nothing* people like to do more than simper up to experts and try to impress them. Then, of course, there are the real experts. What about them? Are you kidding? Real experts always like to share their information with real experts. It is how they show other real experts that they are real experts. It is how they get their rocks off. A real expert will take a gander at your equipment and conclude that you are one of them. That is when modesty will repay you enormously. "Really?" you say. "A what? Where?" That is why you want expensive binoculars. Some real experts do have el-cheapo binoculars or a crummy old pair they got when they were kids and have stuck with ever since, but the reason they have stuck with them ever since is because they are eccentric.†

You shouldn't indulge in expensive binoculars if the sound of them whanging against a rock when you slip and fall backward in pursuit of a Cactus Wren causes you to have a heart seizure, because there is one thing you can count on: you will whang them against a rock.

A rule of thumb: Getting the tiniest little thing repaired on the most expensive binoculars will cost more than it costs to buy a perfectly workable brand-new pair of cheap binoculars. A lot of cheap binoculars, you can run over them with your car and they still work fine.

Look at it this way: there aren't many opportunities for conspicuous consumption in bird-watching, and if that is what turns your crank, go for it.‡ Most of the other opportunities for showing off enormous expenditures have to do with *where* you watch birds. Guatemalan cloud forests being more expensive to get to than city parks.

The other biggie in the realm of equipment is telescopes. Or, if you

---

  * Absolutely nothing. There have been studies.

  † In bird-watching, the line between eccentric and full-tilt wacko is blurred.

  ‡ Binoculars come with a carrying case. Throw it away. If you go around with your binoculars in it, you will look like a dweeb. You are going to look dweebish enough anyway, but even dweeb bird-watchers will think you look like a dweeb.

insist, telescoopoes, the devices through which John Updike discovered it was advantageous to observe birds called "hoopoes."*

You can also spend a bundolo on a scope. Mostly what you do with scopes is watch ducks way out on the water. Before going crazy, ask yourself the following question: How much time do I expect to spend watching ducks way out on the water? Govern your acquisitive desire accordingly. A number of authorities recommend scope powers in the range of 20× or 25×, but another school of thought—the if-I'm-going-to-blow-my-wad-on-a-scope-why-not-get-something-that-will-read-the-sucker's-DNA? school of thought—is inclined toward something with more oomph.

Something to bear in mind, though, is that there is never a time when it is not a total pain in the ass to carry around a scope.† Mainly this is because they are almost always attached to tripods. They are attached to tripods because it is the only way they can be held steady to look at ducks way out on the water because a nut-cutter of a wind will be blowing and it will be so cold the contents of your bladder will have achieved the consistency of a Mr. Frostee. The rest of the time, the weather will not be as good as that. The thing about tripods is that they are always getting busted. A good, sturdy tripod costs a ton. So you've got to ask yourself.

When the answer is yes, you have slipped over the edge.

Birding

"Birding" as a word to describe the activity of watching birds supplanted the term "bird-watching" and "birder" replaced "bird-watcher" because "bird-watching" and "bird-watcher" bring to some minds the image of spinster ladies in tweed underwear bounding through the woods calling "Halloo! Halloo!"‡ They lacked machismo. When bird-

* There *are* birds called "hoopoes." Going to Europe to see them, or, even better, to Africa, is a fine example of conspicuous consumption.

† The best kind of scope is the kind someone else brings along and lets you use.

‡ Not wishing to be sexist, I am, of course, referring to spinster ladies of any gender you care to name.

watching—one hesitates to say, "When bird-watching came out of the closet," but there are only so many metaphors around and some have to do double duty—and moved to the forefront of human activity, it wanted to be known as something that sounded less like "flower arranger" and more like "biker." "Birding" is, however, a dink term. Hunters don't say, "I'm a gooser and I'm going goosing." Or "moosing" or "deering" or "ducking." They are goose hunters or moose hunters or whatever. Or plain hunters. It's been a long time since blasting the living crap out of the feathered friends leavened a day's bird-watching. (Drop around to your local museum. See all the stuffed birds? See all the bird skins in the drawers? The birds stuffed and skinned did not donate their remains to science. They weren't all roadkill.)

When the thrill of the kill went out of bird-watching, what remained sounded a trifle, uh, ineffectual.

"Lemme see if I've got this straight, pardner. You go out in the woods and you look at these itty-bitty birds and you— Whazzat you said? You write down their names? And that's it?"

"Y-y-yessir."

"You hear that, Fat Jake? What say we finish our beers and take this itty-bitty prick out in the parking lot and drive our hogs back and forth over him?"

Bird-watchers needed something that made them sound—or at least made them *think* they sound—like they go out in the woods and spit and belch, and when they fart don't say, "Excuse me." Like they spend a lot of time soaking wet and smelling bad. That is, like guys.

Don't mess with us, we're birders.

Send shivers up your spine? It does with me.

Birdlessness; or Days When You Get the Creepy Feeling That the Only Life Left on the Planet Is You—and You're Not Too Sure About You

A "garbage bird" is a human concept. No bird thinks of itself as a garbage bird. Maybe some should. Ring-billed Gulls, for example. But they don't. That is the point.

There are days when you would give anything to see a Ring-billed Gull. A starling. A part of a starling. You ask yourself, "How can it be there are birds everywhere else on earth except where I am standing at this moment?"

The reasons are:

1. The Ecological Calamity—the end of the biosphere—you have heard so much about has started for good and always, and you happen to be standing at ground zero. Or

2. There are lots of birds around. Everybody is seeing birds but you. This is because you are a jerk.

These feelings will be especially acute if you happen to have taken up bird-watching in the high flush of the spring migration. Then along comes August and the feeling that you are losing your marbles.

Do not despair. This happens to all bird-watchers. There is even an official term for it: These are "Days When There Are No Damn Birds Around."

Book Birding

If you spend time with bird-watchers, something like this will happen before long.

A bird pops up.

You say, "What the hell is that?"

(It is at this point in cute books that the writer makes up a clever bird name.)

"A Rump-teasing Cockledock," the person beside you says right away.

(But this isn't a cute book. This is one tough grunt of a book.)

"A Bendire's Thrasher," the person beside you says right away instead.

"No kidding? I never saw one before."

"Me neither," the person says.

There is a rather pointed pause.

"Then how the hell did you know what it was?"

"I memorized it from the book."

The person standing beside you is a dork. If you didn't realize this before, now you know.

In the best of all possible thickets, the conversation would go like this:

A bird pops up.

You say, "What the hell is that?"

"What? Where? I don't see anything," the person beside you says.

"Over there by the whatchamacallit thing—on the ground there. Stick thing."

"Stick thing?"

"Over there."

"It's some kind of a . . . I don't know. Look in the book."

"I am looking in the— Geez!"

"What?"

"I dropped the book in the slop."

"You dropped your book?"

"Geez!"

"Where'd the bird go?"

"Where'd my book go?"

"The bird! It's gone."

"Those books cost a fortune."

"What do you think it was?"

"It was my bird book."

"No. The bird."

"What do I think the bird was?"

"Yeah."

"Who frigging cares?"

That is an altogether more satisfying sort of person to go bird-watching with. If you happen to be the kind of horrible dork who memorizes birds from the book without ever having seen the real thing, at least do everybody a favor when one of them pops up that nobody can call and keep your mouth shut. Thank you.

Bugs (and Snakes)

Everywhere you go to watch birds there will be bugs that will bite you. A great many of them are deadly.

(It is the same with snakes.)

Besides bugs (and snakes), there are poison oak, poison sumac, poison ivy, and stinging nettles.

With birding, you are taking your life in your hands. There is quicksand. You could get drowned. It was Clementine's involvement with ducklings that led to her demise. Something could fall down and kill you—a tree, a rock. You could fall over something—a bear, a cliff. You could have something in your lunch you are allergic to and you don't even know it until you eat it and have a reaction and die.

Some people say, Why make such a big issue out of all this? It will just make everybody nervous. They're probably right. But is it going to kill you to take a few minutes to make sure your personal affairs are in order before setting out?

Car Cuckoos: On the Road

The thing about watching birds from the car is you know it is a crazy thing to do.

If you're the driver. It is not as crazy as looking up a bird in your field guide while you are at the wheel, hurtling along, but it is still very crazy.

If you've got a passenger, what you are supposed to do is say to your passenger, "Listen, you check out the birds, I'll keep my eye on the road." Sure.

And what is there to see? A flash. A blur. A blip. A streak. A swoosh. A speck way in hell off there. "Whazzat?!"

"*Look out!*" This is your passenger shrieking.

"Immature goshawk? Whaddya think?"

"We just about *died!*" Your passenger is still shrieking, but now he is massaging his chest.

Technical Note: How to perform the Maximum-binders Full-slam Rare-bird-alert Crash-stop.

It cannot be performed properly unless you are considerably in excess of the speed limit. At which point, you or your passenger yell the traditional "Whazzat?!" The difference in this instance is that it is preceded by the key phrase "Holy cow!!"* At which point you: (1) Do not check the rearview mirror. (2) Hit the brakes as hard as you can. (3) Do not signal. (4) Why would you signal? You're not going to pull over, anyway. (5) You're going to stop right there in the middle of the lane and (6) Pay no attention to the fender-bender symphony behind you on the highway.

Properly executed, the Maximum-binders Full-slam Rare-bird-alert Crash-stop will cause more collateral damage than any other bird-watching maneuver.

Car-birding: bird-watching's dirtiest secret. It should be "Don't bird and drive." Drunks might at least look at the road ahead of them every now and then. There's nothing that says they won't. Birders never do.

Cheating

Don't be flashy.

If you go around saying you saw a Scissor-tailed Flycatcher where no one has ever seen one before, you will have to be quick of wit, since the chances of nobody else having seen the one you're claiming to have seen are almost impossible. If there is a Scissor-tailed Flycatcher around, it gets noticed.

---

* Or words to that effect.

You want something that other bird-watchers will give up on after half an hour or so. That eliminates the Ivory-billed Woodpecker. And the Bachman's Warbler. Any vaguely credible (and that "vaguely" can't be overemphasized) report of a Bachman's Warbler will cause several thousand lunatics to spend the rest of their lives within six feet of where it was allegedly seen. They won't even excuse themselves to go to the john.

A Grasshopper Sparrow is perfect. A Grasshopper Sparrow is a bird I personally don't believe exists. I believe everybody who claims to have seen one made it up, but when you get this much intense falsification, it takes on a life of its own, so it even ends up in the field guides. "Somewhat secretive," says *National Geographic*. Right.

Anyway, if you say you saw one ("Gosh, it was there ten minutes ago"), nobody is going to doubt you. (Check your bird maps. If you happened to be standing in northern Saskatchewan when you saw this phantom Grasshopper Sparrow, you will likewise attract more of the sort of attention that you don't care for; the consensus on the imaginary bird is that it doesn't go there, and having to prove that it does will carry you into realms of philosophy where naught but moral acrobats can keep their balance.) In fact, since anybody else who claims to have seen one is living a lie, they will even encourage you. "Have kind of a flat head?" they'll ask. "Flat as pee on a plate," you'll say. "Yup. Had yourself a Grasshopper Sparrow. Wish I'd've seen it. Been a while since I've seen one." They'll scan the field for three seconds and then ooze on out of there.

Differences: It's the Little Things That Make You Nuts

After you have been looking at birds for a while, most of the birds you see will be the birds you most often see. That's all right. You will sigh earnestly and reflect that there are still starlings around, despite the ravages man has unloosed upon the environment. If you get off on that, good for you. Some of us don't. Some of us say, "Look at all the stinking starlings. I can't stand it."

That is a bad attitude. But we keep looking, because what we are looking for is maybe one bird in the midst of the thousands that might not be a starling!*

Six billion Least Sandpipers standing on a mudflat. Maybe one is a Western Sandpiper.

At first, you won't see a lot of difference between a kestrel and a Merlin. You won't at second, either. You won't ever see a lot of Merlins, anyway. Given time, and a bird with not much to do, you can figure out which is which, but often all you get is a blip going past. You have to make do with something other than the marks in the field guides. You need something a shade more metaphysical, even emotional. Here is what the authors of *Hawks in Flight* say: "A Merlin is to a Kestrel what a Harley-Davidson motorcycle is to a scooter." It is a matter of Whammo! (A guy I know says he has no trouble spotting Merlins. He keeps his eye on pigeons. If a pigeon he is watching turns out to be a falcon, it is a Merlin. It sounds screwy, but after you've see a few of them, it starts to make sense. It used to be called a "Pigeon Hawk," but I always thought it was because it killed pigeons. And there *is* something kind of pigeon-headed about Merlins. I am starting to go on and on, aren't I? See what can happen?)

In the first flush of bird-watching, you will spend much of your time trying to figure out the usual stuff that's around. That will keep you busy enough. After you get some idea of that, you will start noticing little differences: something has showed up that isn't usually around.

It is possible to stand near some heronries and see a couple of hundred immature night herons flap in, or flap out. If the *foot and ankle* of every bird that flies by extends beyond the tail, then what you have is a couple of hundred juvenile Yellow-crowned Night Herons. What you want to see then is one that has *only a bit of its foot* sticking out, because then you have a Black-crowned Night Heron. Either that, or a particularly stumpy Yellow-crowned. The differences can be subtle. To some people, it matters a lot which juvenile night heron is which. In time, it may matter to you, too. Then you will have become unbearable.

When the leaves are out and the breezes blow, every little flick of the greenery suggests a bird landing or taking off deep in the cover. Since the

---

* Europe and Africa are filled with beautiful starlings. Some of their most spectacular birds are starlings. They have starlings that knock your eye out.

greenery flicks and flutters a great deal, you will end up being awfully jumpy if you don't soon get over this and start developing some feel for the rhythms of the wind in the trees. Then you will be ready to look for a branch or leaves that are flicking *out* of rhythm. That's the time to start hunting for a bird in the shadows.

Diseases: Diseases You Can Get; Diseases You Can Cause; Whatever

The more you bird, the more birding diseases you are likely to develop. Watch other birders and you will compile an extraordinary list of peculiar ailments in no time. Here are some of the most terrible:

Twitchy Lister Finger. The most pernicious disease of all. An old authority sums up the symptoms this way: "It's as if you hear hoofbeats outside the house and assume a zebra is galloping by." A birder suffering TLF is never in doubt about what a bird is, even if it was nothing but a blur in the twilight. Who is going to argue? You will know you have Twitchy Lister Finger if you see an *Empidonax* flycatcher that is not even as chatty as the Sphinx, and on your list, instead of putting down "*Empidonax* sp?" to indicate that you couldn't figure out what the hell it was, you put a check mark beside "Acadian Flycatcher."

I never come back from seeing so-called peep sandpipers with nothing but "Peep sp?" on my list. I always check off "Least Sandpiper," at least. If I'm going to suffer through the agony of identifying the stupid things *and not be able to figure out a single one*, I deserve a small reward. Some people say this is sort of like a bank teller who has had a bad day taking a little something from the till to cheer himself up. Fine. Whatever gets you through.

Warbler Neck. The bird-watching equivalent of Tennis Elbow. You come down with it because of where most of the warblers are: in the tippety-tops of the trees. This is no joke. It is, however, refreshing to know that every birding ailment is not completely neurotic. With Warbler Neck you can go to the doctor. The doctor will make fun of you, but you can go.

I have a bad case of **Five Minutes Ago**. Any bird worth seeing disappears five minutes before I get there. It is no big deal to see a Purple Sandpiper, but I have never seen one. It is getting upward of forty times that I have showed up someplace where everybody saw Purple Sandpipers five minutes ago.

Crashing. If a bird-watcher saw something good, it takes an age for him to give you all the gory details. I believe this is because when you get right down to it, all he saw was a bird, for God's sake. If he didn't see anything worth mentioning, it can sometimes take an hour to explain how this happened to be so. On top of this, no infinitesimal grain of knowledge is too small to haul out to show your grasp of the subject. Crashing has less to do with the bore a birder is than the headache he can give you.

Dipstick. Related to Crashing, but don't confuse the two. Dipstick is the belief that everybody you meet, whether or not they have expressed any interest at all in birds, would like to hear a great deal about the subject. An extreme form of this is to believe that everyone who happens to bring the subject up (e.g., your boss: "So you were, uh—what is it?—bird-watching on the weekend?") actually wants to be filled in on what you saw.

Spots. As in before your eyes. Those swimmy things—call them whatever you want. Specks. Floaters. Little black dots. They can increase the tallies at a hawk-watch exponentially. A remarkable number of bird-watchers waste a remarkable amount of time trying to see somebody else's spots. A variation of this is schmutz on your lenses.

If you read this section anticipating that it would contain juicy information about the sorts of diseases birds carry and spread, you will be disappointed, but I am sure there are some real beauts. Mao Zedong and his Red Guards were so sure of this they sent all of China on a crusade to kill all the birds. This was to be accomplished by all of China standing under the trees and banging on washbasins with iron spoons, creating such a din that the birds wouldn't land. Unable to land anywhere, the birds eventually would fly themselves to death. The People's Republic gave it their best shot, but it didn't quite work.

A bad bird-watching day isn't necessarily a day when you didn't see any birds. A bad bird-watching day is a day you didn't encounter a birder with some birding disease you had never encountered before. Mind you, maybe you just didn't notice; maybe it is all starting to look normal. Now *that*'s sick.

As far as anybody can tell, no bird-watching diseases are fatal. Except pigeons. Pigeons will kill you.

Fabbydoo Games

In golf, somebody always has a side bet on something or other. For birders, there are not a lot of sideline games apart from getting lost or falling down in a swamp and drowning.

Sometimes, though, somebody will set out to have a "Big Day."

You will be astonished to discover that the object of a Big Day is to see as many species as possible within the twenty-four-hour period. Or at least hear them. Big Dayers spend a lot of time thrashing around in the dark listening for goatsuckers. On a big-deal Big Day* when reputations are at stake, the bird-watchers enlist scouts to check out the country for a couple of days in advance so they will know what to look for and where. There is no dicking around.

A "Big Sit" is easier on the constitution.

You pick a spot and sit there. You count up all the different species you have seen at the end of a given time. You are allowed to use certain aids. A case of beer is a pretty good aid.

And there are birdathons. Some naturalists' group in your area will run a birdathon at some time of the year, you can count on it. Enlist sponsors who will chip in so much per species you find. Rake in millions. Get out of town.

My personal favorite game is how many naked persons I can see while

---

* I spent a couple of days in Africa's Rift Valley, guided by Terry Stevenson not long after he and two other chaps set the world record for Big Days: 342 species on November 30, 1986. Their expedition required five vehicles, two aircraft, and all of Kenya. They failed to see an Olive Thrush, which looks a lot like our robin, behaves like our robin, and is as common as our robin. (I mention this not merely to name-drop, but because I wrote the trip off on my income taxes under "research.")

on a bird-watching expedition. Since years can go by without seeing any, when one does spring into focus, I consider it a Big Day.

But don't go away from this thinking that birding is an endless succession of fabbydoo games or fun, fun, fun without a moment's rest. Quite the opposite. Birding is mostly looking at birds. It is no use trying to pretend otherwise.

Field Guides

"It is a truth universally acknowledged that a beginning birdwatcher in possession of a good pair of binoculars, must be in want of a field guide." —Jane Austen

But which one?

It is a big question, because we are talking about *the* book—small enough for you to carry into the field, hence the name "field guide"; clever people these woodsy folks—that will tell you what the hell the bird is you're watching. If the guide you choose gives you troubles, everything from there on is a long, wet slog. And there are a lot of choices.

Not least is how the guide is illustrated. Some field guides use paintings, some use photographs. At the outset, it may seem to you that photographs will make identification easier. That would be your first mistake.

Hard as it is to imagine, every House Sparrow looks different to every other House Sparrow.* Although these variations seem slight to us, they can have a substantial effect on what we see. Photographs always show a specific—that is, unique—individual. Field guide paintings don't; they are generalizations, and draw attention to the most noteworthy similarities within a species.

So don't use a field guide illustrated with photographs to get yourself started. If you go along and the craziness sets in, you will acquire lots of

---

* To a House Sparrow, we all look alike.

field guides, some illustrated with photographs so you can split hairs. Fine. But for the moment, you've got enough problems.

Among field guides illustrated with paintings (we are talking smallish paintings; not the Sistine Chapel), there are, at the moment, three main contenders:

Roger Tory Peterson's various volumes, the National Geographic Society's *Field Guide to the Birds of North America,* and Golden Press's *Birds of North America: A Guide to Field Identification*, generally known as the Golden guide.

First, a word about Roger Tory Peterson. Roger Tory Peterson is a genius. His genius depends not even slightly on his fabulous ability to paint wildlife, or his sumptuous photography, or his vast (isn't that enough already?) abilities as a writer. It has to do with little arrows. He invented little arrows. He invented them and sprinkled them on his field guide illustrations to bring our attention to key field marks. This is known as the "Peterson System."*

It is a doozy.

The smartest move you can make starting out is to buy the Peterson guide for your neck of the woods. The first time you see a bird, you will have a bad-enough time figuring out what it is, even with a field guide.† Peterson gives you a leg up by telling you at a glance the one, two, or at the very most three things about each species that set it apart. His text has a nice, personal, folksy touch: nothing too intimidating about it. It is well organized. He quickly describes species that are similar, and their most obvious differences, and his descriptions of the songs are logical and kind of funky.

The drawback is that the text details are sometimes a shade skimpy, although the prose is invariably livelier than any of the others.

You may stick happily with him forever, but after a while, you may

---

* Before this, bird-watchers were reduced to pointing. Considering where a bird-watcher's finger might have been, this was hardly sanitary.

† The thing that makes you certifiable is the two-hundred-thousandth time you have seen the, for instance, female House Sparrow, and you can't figure out what the goddamn thing is. Okay, so the light was bad. But it is the sort of thing the birders you hang around with will never forget. The real question is, How come you hang around with such total pricks?

want something with a bit more heft. If you do, the National Geographic is far and away the best. The illustrations are big, and for tricky species there are plenty of them, showing all sorts of plumages. And the paintings are a shade more subtle, less showy, than Peterson's; somehow more natural.

The text tends to be dense and detailed. Often, there is too much to take in on the spur of the moment. Often, it includes little points that you sort of wish had leapt out at you at the time. But, unlike Peterson, the maps are right there on the same page and a lot of the calls you make are pure mapwork.

The Golden guide was around long before the National Geographic's, but even expanded and revised, it has never quite caught up. Things are too jammed together, the illustrations are too small. The Golden boasts one of the weirdest features in bird-dom. Sonograms. Birdsongs transcribed on little graphs, in something like lie detector squiggles or electrocardiograms. I don't know anybody who has the foggiest notion of what they mean.

When you do launch into photographically illustrated guides, check out *The Audubon Society Master Guide to Birding*. It comes in three volumes and can be very useful as long as you have a forklift to carry it around.

How to Use a Field Guide

Identifying a bird is easy. All you have to do is look it up in your field guide. It is the looking up that is hard.

You see a bird you have never seen before. Unless it is an alien space mutant or has blown in from Sumatra on a hurricane, it is in the field guide you're flipping through.

The laws of bird-watching now come into play.

Law One: You have only seen the bird for two-tenths of a second.

Law Two: It will take you twenty minutes (or maybe two hours; anyway, too long) to find it in the book. And then, unless it is something unmistakable like a Great Kiskadee, or enormous like an American White Pelican, you won't be even slightly sure that what the book shows and what you saw are the same thing.

Finding your way through a field guide can be as maddening as finding your way through the great outdoors in search of the genuine article. I hate to sound tight-assed, but it is worth taking a bit of time and figuring out how the field guide is organized.* At first, even this won't make a tremendous amount of sense because the guide isn't arranged by color or by size or by all sorts of what you might think of as obvious ways. But there is rhyme and reason to it, and after ten or twenty years, it will fall into place. You still won't be able to find what you saw in there, but you will realize it isn't the book that is stupid.

The field guides have very nice introductions—sometimes called "How to Use This Book"—that tell you precisely that. All three provide useful maps of the bird's own topography so that you need never again fail to know where to look for the scapular and where for the axillars.

From there on, the books are laid out roughly the same. There are minor variations, but they all start with loons, then grebes, and they all end up with songbirds. When you get a bird list for your region or for some particular wildlife sanctuary, it will be organized along these same basic lines. The reason is scientific; it is the way birds are generally thought to have evolved. The loons being the most primitive, the sparrows and finches—that is, the songbirds—the least. This order is known as phylogenetic,† and, besides, you have to start somewhere.

Now what you do is milk the book for clues, and not just eye-ring or no eye-ring, wing bar or no wing bar.

One Good Clue: Look at the map. If you think you have found a Clark's Nutcracker and you are standing at the southern tip of Florida, a glance at the Clark's Nutcracker map will show you that you might be mistaken. You might not be, but at least you should do a bit more investigating.

Another Good Clue: What is the bird in the picture doing? The artists often try to put them in something like their normal habitat, and in a relatively distinctive pose. Ducks are swimming, eagles are not. (Although anybody who has seen a bunch of eagles in the vicinity of a salmon run has seen them land on fish swimming near the surface and paddle— using their wings as paddles—their catch ashore. Any damned thing is possible.) The Connecticut Warblers are strutting their stuff. The point

---

* RYFM is the advice given to computer hysterics who have been knocked for a loop by a hitherto (they believe) unheard of glitch. "RYFM" stands for "Read your effing manual."

† It brings to mind Haeckel's crack about ontogeny recapitulating phylogeny.

being that if a bird is shown strolling around on the ground, it is more likely to be a towhee than a chickadee.

If you see a bird climbing around on the trunk of the tree pecking at the bark, you can say, Aha! Woodpecker! But when you thumb through the woodpeckers, the bird you saw in your binoculars doesn't look like any of them. Check out the nuthatches, then. Also the Brown Creeper. They likewise are shown clambering around on the tree trunks, pecking bugs out of the interstices or whatever. What? Not a nuthatch? Not a creeper? Then, holy gazonga! You've got an alien space— Wait! Is the bird kind of stripy, black and white? Eventually, you will come upon the Black-and-White Warbler. A warbler that acts as if it is halfway between a woodpecker and a nuthatch. If you have the Golden guide I dumped on a while back, you will even have a picture of it clambering around on a tree trunk. In the other guides, you have to divine this unusual (for a warbler) habit from the text.

The first few times you take field guide in hand and look for the bird you have just seen, you won't know which way to turn. It is confusing as hell. Gradually, though, you will see that sparrows look different than flycatchers look different than thrushes look different than wrens. They have different shapes. They have different postures. They act differently. These things, in time, will tell you not to go blindly through the whole book, but to look under thrushes or sparrows or whatever. This doesn't always work. Some birds were sent to try us. Not even all Song Sparrows look the same.* But eventually, you will more or less catch on. And if you don't, by carefully using *this* book—*Down & Dirty Birding*—you will be able to fake it.

---

* There are thirty-one subspecies of Song Sparrow. All peep sandpipers look the same, though. I don't care what anybody says.

Hawk-watching

"I am but mad north-northwest: when the wind is southerly I know a hawk from a handsaw." —*Hamlet, claiming he hasn't lost all his marbles*

Watching hawks is a distinct diversion. It is one of two kinds of birding that take place only during migration. The other kind is candy-assed birding. Anybody can watch birds when birds are migrating because they are all over the place; the sky is full of them, the trees are full of them, you trip over them, you have to shoo them out of the way. Birding in February, *that's* what separates serious birders from the candy-asses.

It is quite possible to hunt up hawks and watch them all year round, but that is not what is meant by "hawk-watching." "Hawk-watching" means standing around waiting for the hawks to come to you. This can be more difficult than it sounds. Sometimes, they are no more than little wee dots you can hardly see with even the most powerful binoculars. Sometimes, you run out of coffee.

Some hawk-watchers get out in even the foulest weather. These are known as "dumb-assed hawk-watchers," since hawks don't much bother to migrate except when the weather is reasonable. "Reasonable" doesn't mean even drizzling slightly. Hawks don't much like to get up early in the morning either, or to work late in the day. This gives hawk-watching considerable appeal.

Die-hard hawk-watchers call other birds "dickey birds," and the birders who watch them "dickey-bird watchers." That gives you a pretty good idea of their point of view. For hawk-watchers, garbage birds start with Whooping Cranes. Hawk-watching can be extremely social, as birding goes. Watches are held at regular sites (the best ones are sites that hawks go by), and generally are dressed up with some fancy, important-sounding purpose such as gossiping. For this reason, hawk-watching is a whole lot noisier than most birding. On top of that, hawk-watchers often interrupt their chitchat and call out the hawks that are passing to make sure the counters enter the correct data on the census sheets, and to impress the other watchers with their astonishing ability to identify microscopic dots a mile up.

If the idea that hawks often appear as little tiny dots a long, long way off seems to be running through this like a thread, it is because when the Broad-winged Hawks are migrating, for example, sometimes they do it in flocks of thousands upon thousands, and sometimes these flocks are so high up that with the barenaked eye you would never have the slightest idea they were there. Sometimes, though, they are higher than that. Watchers estimate the numbers with great care, making sure to add in all the little dots floating in their eyes, and multiplying by their area code.

In certain conditions, the hawks can be much closer. Sometimes close enough to identify some of the field marks unique to the various birds of prey. Sometimes closer still. When a Golden Eagle booms over at treetop height, or when a Peregrine Falcon rips past fifty feet away, hawk-watchers have what they call "a complete orgasm."

Life List

It is very cool not to know what the total is exactly.

Somebody asks, "How many on your life list?"

Now, one thing you do know is precisely how many birds are on your life list. Not only that, you can name every one of the suckers by memory; name them and say where it was you saw them, whether they were right-handed or left-handed, what the weather was like, whether they were up-sun or down, what you were wearing, and what you had for breakfast. Spouses you might be a little vague on; not life birds.

But what you say is, "I dunno. Maybe eight hundred or so."

"*You don't know how many exactly?!*"

"Nah. I don't keep too close track."

Leaving the other person thinking, He's seen almost exactly the same number of species as there have ever been found on the whole entire continent* and he doesn't even bother keeping too close track. He must be some kind of Bird-watching God.

At some point, even a Bird-watching God has to confront a mortal question: What to include on your life list? And at some point, you will

---

* I don't think I've seen anywhere near that many.

encounter some bird-watching geezer who will say, "Every birder keeps their own life list."

Meaning you can put any damned thing on it you want.

Since you are the only person who much cares about it, you can be as scrupulous as you care to be, or not.

For the scrupulous, the general rules tend to be:

Dead birds. Nope.

Caged ones, neither. There goes everything in the aviary at the zoo.

The same goes for domestic birds. There are loads of Mandarin Ducks in North America, some living quite happily in the wildwood, or at least in park ponds. They are referred to as "escapes." Almost certainly every one of them has escaped from somebody's stock of imported scenic birdlife.

At some point, all sorts of domestic and pet-type birds have got free and got to breeding and established themselves as actual species in the wild. The Mute Swan, for instance. It has earned an authorized place on the list. Who is to say the European Goldfinch at my backyard feeder hasn't done the same thing? Nobody. As the geezer says, you keep your own list. If you want to keep some parts of it secret, there's no law against it.

Trapped birds. If you hang around bird-banders with their nets, you will sometimes see something rare and astonishing plucked from the strands. Can this be counted? A scrupulous life-lister says, Not unless it is still here and flying around loose twenty-four hours later.

I am painfully scrupulous. I don't like to put a bird on my life list until I see it well enough that I will recognize one if I see it again. I want the whole bird, down pat—as opposed to nothing but a view of the Mangrove Cuckoo's tail feathers deep in the shadows and no way of getting a better look because of the snakes. On the other hand, if something blasts overhead and all I see is a flash and some hotshot calls out "Gyrfalcon!" my position is this: I didn't get what you would call "a good look," I'm not even sure it was a bird, it could've been some kind of flying beaver, but there is a good chance I will never see a Gyrfalcon again in my whole life, so screw it. I put Gyrfalcon on my life list.

This seems to me to be a balanced approach.

Listing

For those of you who want bird-watching to be a blood sport, this is where it happens. Here you wallow in the worst aspects of the human spirit.

Listing—the insatiable urge to see as many kinds of birds as is humanly possible, as opposed to keeping simple track of birds that you have seen—is to bird-watching what Michael Milken was to collecting extra pennies in a jar. North Americans call it "listing"; the British call it "twitching." "Twitching" is a better word because it is what people who do it do. You can pick them out in a crowd. You can pick them out in a satellite photograph.

A lister is interested in just one thing: numbers.

And in one kind of numbers: big.

Don't misunderstand this. Everyone keeps a list. Without a list, how would you remember what you saw? And it is the most natural thing in the world to tally this list up at the *HOLY GAZONGA! I HAVE SEEN A HUNDRED AND TWELVE SPECIES SINCE BREAKFAST!!!* end of the day, but that doesn't make us "listers" any more than appreciating the way another person fills out their shirt makes us sex deviates.

When two listers meet, the conversation goes like this:

"How many species you got today?"

"A hundred and twelve."

"Is that all? You poor sad excuse for a piece of human . . ."

They know perfectly well that this actuarial mania strips bird-watching of its beauties, its connection with nature, of the perspective it gives mankind on our place in the cosmos. They don't care.

". . . excrement."

When two of the far-more-sensitive, nonlisting sorts of bird-watchers meet, the conversation takes a more aesthetic course.

"I saw the most glorious Magnolia Warbler flitting through the budding—"

"How many species you got today?"

"A hundred and twelve."

"Is that all? You poor sad excuse for a piece of human . . ."

Wait a minute. Something's gone dreadfully wrong here.

". . . excrement."

A bird comes in many denominations of listing value.

Take a Red-winged Blackbird. By every estimate, there are more Red-winged Blackbirds in North America than any other kind of bird.

But if you have never seen one before, the first one you lay eyes on is your *life bird*.

If it is the first Red-wing you have seen returning after winter, it is a *year bird*.

If you are on a bird-watching trip, the first Red-wing you see will be a *trip bird*.

The first one you see the next day will be a *day bird*.

If you have seen 385 Red-wings already today, the next one you see will be a *garbage bird*. So were the preceding 384.

As there are many bird denominations, so there are many species of list.

My wife has a *television list*. I have a *subway list*. Subway birding is a challenge because it is hard to get the driver to stop the train when you see something that looks as if it might be good if you could get a few minutes to check it out thoroughly.

Missing the Call

It is very difficult to screw up if you keep your mouth shut.

But if you are even slightly intent on demonstrating your (growing) expertise, you won't keep your mouth shut. You will rush in where even fools tread carefully.

Good. Bird-watchers don't have much else to enliven their evenings but recollections of legendary bad calls.

As you go along, you will discover certain truths:

A female House Sparrow all on its own in some remote locale—well, the last thing you expect to see there is a female House Sparrow. So it is the last thing you think of. And by the time you think of it, you're liable to have called it something real dumb. Believe me.

Mourning Doves. Nine times out of ten, Mourning Doves look like something else first. Something exotic. Even more exotic than Merlins. Something that will make you sound like a complete goddamn fool if you shout it out as soon as the bird wings into view.

Female Red-winged Blackbirds are real pains in the ass for the first few weeks after they come back in the spring; until your eye gets used to them.

Everybody has their own list of booby-trapped birds.

Part of the fun of hanging around with experts is watching them miss a call. It's the kind of thing that can make you feel good all over.

Don't, on the other hand, be so shy that a promising bird that everyone else has overlooked skedaddles because you were reluctant to point it out. "Look at that thing! What is it?" is a nice, workable approach. The fate of nations does not rest on bird-watching, despite what some birders will tell you.

Miss Slinger's Everyday Birdiquette

Don't be a jerk. It all boils down to that.

This jerk dictum isn't universally accepted by any means. And not just because it is one of those concepts that always seems to apply a whole lot more to thee than to me.

In too many minds, there is a notion that the act of bird-watching, by definition, demonstrates a deep and abiding kinship with, and respect for, nature and all things in it, and as a result, anyone who is watching birds is lifted beyond earthly constraints and is free to engage in any kind of brain-dead behavior they care to.

This has always been a problem, but now it is worse because so many more bird-watchers are out and about. At the same time, there are fewer places to go to see birds. And maybe fewer birds to see.

Here are some rules. People who violate them are jerks—really, they could be issued with official jerk documents.

🏴 Stay back. From birds, from nests. That's one reason you have binoculars.

🏴 Don't take flash pictures. If you've got the kind of equipment that allows you to take decent pictures without a flash, you don't have to get very close at all.

🏴 Most little birds can't hear much of the human voice. Most bird-watchers can. Talk softly. Keep your ears open. You will be astonished what you will hear if you shut up. And you won't hear any birds unless you do.

🏴 Birds do tend to notice sudden, sharp movements. Go gently, smoothly. Don't point, as in "It's right there, *see?!!*" Because it won't be, any longer.

🏴 Pishing (see "Pishing") is all right within limits. So are other birdcalls, if you can make them. But don't use tapes. Tapes ultimately can chase away whatever it is you are trying to attract. And they make other birders homicidal.

🏴 Don't flush birds. If a bird doesn't want to come out and get watched, it probably has a good reason. It might be scared. It might be hurt. It might plain not give a flying fadoodle about ending up on your list. It is already having a hard time making its way in a difficult world. Give it a break.

🏴 Stay off private land without permission. The grand old excuse—"We're bird-watchers"—is wearing so thin it is liable to get your buns filled with buckshot. People are touchy these days. Considering the way bird-watchers sometimes think they own the scenery, it is not without cause. Close gates. Don't see if you can get the cows to stampede.

🏴 If there is a path, stay on it. A single pebble can fall without a sound, a million pebbles can be an avalanche.

🏴 Don't drop cigarette butts. Don't drop nasal tissues. Don't drop anything. Not even names. (Fat chance.)

All this can be summed up quite simply. Don't be a jerk.

Niagara: Metaphor for Hell

Some things cannot be explained adequately. Every region has its equivalent. It might be the desert in high summer. The rain forest in the rain. A godawful place to be, but a bird-watcher's gotta do what a bird-watcher's gotta do.

The Niagara River: falls, rapids, whirlpool, gorge; a wonder no tourist should miss. But it is only of interest to birders when no tourist in his right mind would be out-of-doors, much less roaming up and down the wind-torn edges of the cliffs above the mist. What they are looking for is gulls. They are looking for them in the hind end of November, a time of the year that is listed in *Webster*'s under "misery." That is the only time you encounter the gull phenomenon, a unique and unexplainable congregation. On a good day (a birding term having everything to do with numbers and nothing to do with comfort), you can see maybe thirteen species of gull along the river, more than you can see together anywhere else on the continent, maybe in the world.

"See" isn't the right word for most of us. Imagine a blizzard of gulls. You are way up here, the blizzard is a couple of hundred feet down there in the bottom of a canyon. One billion of the snowflakes (the blizzard and snowflakes are metaphorical, and not to be confused with the real blizzard and snowflakes that are whistling around you) are Ring-billed Gulls. But there are one billion and one snowflakes. The other one is a Black-legged Kittiwake. With any kind of luck at all, it will be around for five minutes.

Something to remember about the fabulous excitement this creates: Go due east eight hundred miles and you will be up to your yingyang in Black-legged Kittiwakes. Birding possesses its own theory of relativity.

Ornithologist

Don't call yourself one unless you are one. If you do, somebody will ask you about the endocrine system. Then what do you say?

Pishing, and Other Methods of Attracting Birds Without Abandoning All Redeeming Social Values

It is called "pishing." Don't blame me.

You make the sound by saying, "*Pssssssshhhhhhhhhhhhhhhhhhhhhhh.*"

That is, you drop the *i*. You can leave the *i* in if you want and say, "*Pisssssssshhhhhhhhhhhhhhhhhhhhhhh.*" But you already sound ridiculous enough.

The theory is that the noise—you repeat it a few times, dramatically—sounds something like the distress calls little birdies make *in extremis*. Naturally, if something is attacking a little birdy, and the little birdy makes a distress call, all the other little birdies rush to get a look at what is going on. The fact that this theory doesn't make any sense makes it a particularly good one. If you or I were a little birdy and we heard a distress call, we might say to ourselves, "Sounds like time we got the hell out of here."

I have pished, and I have watched energetic pishers at work. I have seen screw-all of note turn up as a result. Now, that's not exactly true. Black-throated Blue Warblers find it all very interesting, and American Redstarts. So do chickadees, and on a dreary day in the shank of the year, a chickadee can strike a spark in your hearth like nothing else on earth.

Squeaking. There is a squeaking kind of noise you can make by kissing the back of your hand. Some people kiss the back of their hand, some sophisticated birders kiss the backs of the hands of others. Some kiss a knuckle. Some people think this causes birds to chirp in response. It is a change from pishing. That alone is a commendation.

Gizmos. Every bird-type store you go into sells squeaking gizmos. Usually, these are thimble-sized wooden things made of some impressive kind of wood. Inside is a metal-type thing with a sort of key handle that you turn. This produces a squeaking sound. Even more pronounced is the sharp chipping sound it can make. Almost always, the package this squeaker comes in contains a little capsule containing something like rosin. You sprinkle this inside the gizmo to make it squeak better. By the time you get home at the end of the first day, you have lost the little rosin capsule. The next time you go out birding, you will not be able to find the squeaker gizmo itself. That is because you forgot to look in your dresser drawer. It is in there beside the squeaker gizmo you bought a year ago and forgot about. Some veteran bird-watchers have a half dozen of them in the same drawer.

Clicking Two Pebbles Together. There is a belief that the sound of two pebbles being clicked together will cause Yellow Rails to call out. Their call is almost always described as being "like the sound of two pebbles clicking together." You are in for a real disappointment if you spend a lot of time clicking pebbles together and there is no water anywhere in sight. It's not something you can just go out in the backyard and do to any good effect. If anything calls for the right habitat, this does.

Imitating a Screech Owl. I believe I imitate the sound of a screech owl rather well. Nobody else believes I do, and it doesn't impress any birds that I have noticed, but it gives me a sense of accomplishment, and that is enough.

Other people who imitate screech owls report that when they do it, small birds fly up with the idea of mobbing the owl and chasing it away. It must be something to see.

Tapes. I have been on hand several times when playing a tape of a screech owl has caused another screech owl to ghost in to see what the hell is going on. Scant pages ago, I somewhat sharply criticized people who use tapes to attract birds because, in the long run, it doesn't do the birds any good, and in the short run, the amplified noise drives other bird-watchers out of their skulls. But, hey, sometimes there's nobody else around. And sometimes you might have good, sound scientific reasons for playing a tape, such as you need a screech owl to put on your day's list and haven't been able to find one and now it is dark. There is enough about bird-watching that is tight-assed without going overboard.

Pronunciation:
You Can Walk the Walk, but Can You Talk the Talk?

So you won't sound like a complete yutz. Most bird names are pronounced like you'd expect. How else are you going to say "Yellowlegs"? "Three-toed Woodpecker"? "Worm-eating Warbler"? But some might throw you for a loop.

Anhinga. An-HING-ga.

Ani. AH-knee.

Avocet. AH! vo-set.

Dowitcher. Years ago in Canada, there was a brand of beer called Dow. Its advertising line was the grammar grabber: "Wouldn't a Dow Go Good Now?" Think Dow Corning. It's as if you were saying "dowager."

Egret. EEEE-gret. Yee-haw!

Eider. EYE-der. Like the eiderdown on the bed.

Gallinule. GAL(like the one that married dear old whatsisname)-in-yule.

Gannet. The newspaper chain is gah-NET. The bird is GAN-ut.

Glaucous Gull. GLOCK-us.

Guillemot. Forestall Frenchification. GWIL-uh-mott.

Gyrfalcon. When Yeats wrote, "Turning and turning in the widening gyre/The falcon cannot hear the falconer," he was under the impression that "gyre" was pronounced as if it were "jire." As in, whilst watching the hootchy-kootchy dancer, one becomes aware of her gyrations. What did Yeats know? Bird-watchers pronounce it "jeer." JEER-falcon.

Ibis. EYE-bis.

Jaeger. In North America, we pronounce the J. Europeans make it a Y. JAY-ger. YAY-ger.

Magnificent Frigatebird. Not fri-GATE bird. Remember that quaint old saying "Frig it"? Like that.

Merganser. Mer-GAN-zer.

Murre. And they brought him gold, frankincense, and a murre. Yea, and the bird smelled powerfully fishy.

Northern Parula. Puh-ROO-luh.

Osprey. OSS-pray.

Phalarope. FAL(rhymes with pal)-a-rope.

Phoebe. FEE-bee.

Pied-billed Grebe. Not *pee-edd* as if it was the French for foot. Think of the Pied Piper. Pied beds. Pie-eyed.

Pileated. You can get into arguments over this one, but most commonly PILLY-ate-ed.

Plover. Not PLOE as in BLOW, goddammit. Pluvver. Rhymes with lover.

Prothonotary Warbler. Pro-THON-uh-tary.

Ptarmigan. The *P* is silent. As in pswimming. (Psorry.)

Pyrrhuloxia. PEER(then say everything after that as if it were only one syllable)-uhluxya. And good luck to ya. It might be easier, if there's one around, just to keep your eyes closed. If you don't see it, you don't have to call it.

Roseate Spoonbill. Roseate Tern. Rosy ate.

Ruffed Grouse. Sometimes it looks mighty ruffled, but it ain't Ruffled.

Rufous (Hummingbird, Towhee). ROO-fuss.

Sandwich Tern. You hear samwitch. You hear sangwidge. You hear all sorts of things.

Scaup. As ugly as a word can get. Skop.

Skua. SKOO-uh.

Vireo. VEE-ree-oh.

X-TREE-mly ob-SESS-uv com-PUL-suv, or what? It goes with the territory.

Rarities, or
Oh, Christ, There's Something Amazing in My Yard

What if it's not?

What if it *is*?

What if it never shows up again?

When it comes to rare birds, there are two things you want to think about very carefully.

1. Letting on that you've seen one.

2. Letting on that you've got one in your yard.

Most of the time, a rare bird is a relative matter. A rare bird in California may be one that is common as dirt in Winnipeg.

If you hear from other bird-watchers, or learn on the local hotline that there is a rare bird in your vicinity, go. You may never make it to Winnipeg and this is your chance.

The thing can get very knotty, though. For instance, when you are the one who finds the rare bird. If you find it, then you want to get the word out as quickly as possible so somebody else will see it and verify that you are neither deluded nor a moron. Or do you? What if, by the time you get the word out, the bird has flown?

Then you will be subjected to close scrutiny.* You will have to fill out a rare bird report. You will be questioned in such a fashion as makes the Inquisition seem like heavy petting. The chances that you will end up sounding like a complete horse's patoot are enormous. Remember: Everyone who grills you is bent out of shape because they didn't see the bird (*if* it existed) and their greatest interest is not in helping you add another entry to your life list. They are intent on proving that you are such a doofus that they didn't miss anything at all. It is something to bear in mind.

The other thing to think about is: What if the bird shows up in your yard? What if it doesn't just show up, but visits your feeder every twenty minutes, as regularly as a city bus? What if you're not even that much of a bird-watcher, you just figured something out of the ordinary was out there and mentioned it to somebody who mentioned it to somebody?

Well, it's your funeral. And your furniture, and your garden. You may get your jollies out of all the attention. Who knows?

---

* When they used to burn witches, the burnee's last gasp often was "Compared to turning in a rare bird report, this is a day at the beach."

Sewage Lagoons

Another ghastly truth about bird-watching.

Before we go much further, something must be cleared up. If the word "lagoon" creates in your mind a vision of palm trees, blue waters, breakers out at the reef, shimmering sands, bare flesh swaying to the sensuous strains of a ukulele, you are going to be surprised by your first sight of a sewage lagoon.* Also by your first whiff.

Sewage lagoons are always posted. Nobody is allowed through the gate except authorized personnel, and if this is what being authorized personnel gets you, it is enough to cause a sensible person to seek some other career path. It is one birder in ten thousand who has authorization to get in to see a sewage lagoon. That means all the rest either have to climb over the fence or crawl under it. In other words, they must commit an illegal act. They do.

They do because birds love sewage lagoons.

They also do because there aren't many terrible difficulties a bird-watcher must overcome. One of them is being in circumstances that are intolerable to any other human being in any other circumstances. It is sort of a birder's machismo. Or, since bird-watching is gender neutral, mystique.

Sometimes after spending a couple of hours around a sewage lagoon on a stinking hot, humid day with the sweat pouring down their bodies like they were standing under a firehose turned up full volume, birders will preserve this mystique by not having a bath for another two or three days. Other birders who encounter them will acknowledge this invisible mark of honor by retching in admiration.

The steamier the day, and the stiller the air, the better the birding at the old sewage lagoon. This is because birds flying overhead are overcome and pitch, unconscious, into it. Or maybe they just like the feel of sewage between their toes.

---

* I am up to maybe my fiftieth or sixtieth and I am still surprised.

Too Much

Sadly, there are almost no put-downs exclusive to birding. Every other human endeavor has a list of delicious words and phrases that allow the seasoned veteran to crap all over a novice (cowboys have their greenhorns), or to dismiss a colleague's abilities (I am a writer, you are a hack).

Birding spent so long being polite that it hasn't yet developed a satisfactory pejorative vocabulary beyond the usual run of A-words, B-words, C-words, and so on.

I have encountered one very nasty comment, however, that, as dumps go, rates with the greatest anywhere.

Said—behind the back, of course, and with weary disdain—of some blowhard who has boasted of accomplishments that seem barely credible:

"He sees too much."

It is a lovely notion from every angle. More vicious it is scarcely possible to get with mere speech. Try it the first chance you get. It will make you feel better.

Tough Calls

Every reputable field guide tells you what it is about the looks of the Black-capped Chickadee that sets it apart from the Carolina Chickadee. If you read carefully, though, there's always a hedge. Even in the hand— expert birders set a lot of store by what you can see examining a bird "in the hand"*—only an expert who is extremely full of himself will tell you which is which. The most useful distinction has nothing to do with appearance. It is song; they don't sing the same way. But—and this is an extremely good "but"—what if they don't happen to be singing? Here is one thing you can do: Look at the distribution maps in the bird guide. If

* Another exclusionary bit of business. Who else but experts and extremely sick individuals spend any amount of time with a bird in their hand?

you are standing in Black-capped country,* what you are looking at is most likely a Black-capped. If it is Carolina country, you've got a Carolina. If you are in an area where overlap is likely, you don't know what the hell you've got. And neither does anybody else. So forget it.

The wise thing is to err on the side of common sense.

On the other hand, you can call it anything you want. If you want to stand in the middle of South Dakota and report a Carolina Chickadee, nobody is likely to argue with you. For one thing, nobody else is probably going to be able to find the bird, since chickadees have a way of disappearing into the crowd. What they will do instead is never believe another thing you report. Behind your back, they will call you a goof.

Other tough calls: The *Empidonax*—another word bird-watchers throw around to give themselves airs†—flycatchers are easy enough to tell apart by song. The thing is, they spend most of their lives not singing. Nevertheless, there are smart-ass birders who claim to be able to distinguish the species by sight. Maybe they can. But ask yourself this: What kinds of lives do they lead?

There are fine distinctions among the peep sandpipers in winter plumage. What that means is that if you want to go to the trouble of figuring them out, fine.‡

Yellowlegs. There is the Greater and there is the Lesser. If you see just one and it is keeping its mouth shut, then you don't know which one it is unless you are a genius or a liar. If you see a whole bunch, all roughly the same size, the same applies. If you see a bunch, some shorter, with a thinner, straighter bill than the taller ones that have bills angling up just a shade and knees that are knobblier, what you probably have is an agglomeration of Greater and Lesser Yellowlegs. You can write it down in your book. But it is still a guess.

Even more of a guess is Short-billed versus Long-billed Dowitchers.

---

* This works only if you know where you are at that moment. Mark Twain said there is only one requirement for training a dog, and that is that you be smarter than the dog. For some reason, this strikes me as relevant.

† It means little grayish, brownish, yellowish pains in the ass.

‡ I don't mean to boast, but I can see a couple of hundred peep sandpipers in winter plumage skittering around on a mudflat and be perfectly happy that I realize they're not ducks. Beyond that, whatever they care to be is up to them.

Scientific studies have found that some Short-billed Dowitchers have bills longer than Long-billed Dowitchers. So who knows? Who really knows?

Things get very tricky between the Cooper's Hawks and the Sharp-shinned Hawks. Thanks to the females of both species being much larger than the males, you get a bewildering middle ground where the female Sharpie is often the same size as, and sometimes even bigger than, the male Cooper's. This can lead to bracing discussions in the field.

This discussion of tough calls doesn't begin to consider the "Confusing Fall Warblers." Some people have the kind of neurotic minds that can keep all the warblers in their autumn plumages straight. Some of us don't. We say, "Stuff it," and wait for spring. If you want to drive yourself crazy, though, go ahead.

What to Wear

It comes down to how much of a dork you want to look like. Some people can never get too much of a good thing.

Americans like belonging to dorky majorities. They are terrific joiners, or if not, they like to appear as if they are terrific joiners.* The distinguishing feature of an American bird-watcher is a badge, or a crest, and never just one of either. Are you kidding? They appear in the woods as a mosaic of memberships, walking testimonials to involvement. Whether it matters what the badges or crests represent is not clear. The hierarchy of birding associations in the United States is not something shared with foreigners. Some of the more impressive American university degrees come from numbered post office boxes in Nevada, and it could be the same holds true for naturalist associations. But an American birder would no more bird without visible bona fides than blow his nose on Old Glory.

Canadians tend to be independently dorky. If they do belong to anything, they would never let on in public because then you would want to join, too, and the last person they would want in their organization is

* *E pluribus unum* and all that jazz.

anyone of your sort. There would go the exclusivity.* When garments began to appear that had, fashionably, the labels on the outside, Canadian birders worried that this would indicate some leanings or other and avoided wearing them, or wore them only when they birded at night, when there was little chance of this affiliation being noticed.

One of the problems facing the fashion-conscious birder is that no particular gear is required, apart from binoculars. Almost every other human endeavor calls for some sort of significant or identifiable costume: this is often the reason people take it up in the first place; they like the look. Soccer boots and kneesocks suit some women better than ballet slippers and tutus. Some men, too, no doubt. Gardeners get their own custom-designed *gloves*. But for bird-watchers, whatever you're wearing is perfectly all right, and without a recognizable costume you quickly come to the realization that by walking around with binoculars slung from your neck you can easily be taken for a pervert.

Camouflage gear has become big with hunters, who have problems of their own to begin with, and big with U.S. birders. It is regarded by some as the sort of thing that separates the "birder" from the "bird-watcher." Camouflage gear might be useful when it comes to keeping Bambi from spotting an ambush, but with birds, it doesn't have any effect one way or another. Birds, especially the rarely seen kind from isolated realms, are not likely to be any more disturbed by humankind barging into their habitat than they would be if a gopher did. Or a moose. Some things strike them as predators, some things don't. If you go into the woods dressed like a Sharp-shinned Hawk, you might have trouble finding any other bird that hasn't headed for the hills. But a bird that isn't bothered by a moose is hardly going to be bothered by you in your everyday rat-bag outfit, provided you behave the way the moose does, which is relatively low-key. A moose in rut is a different matter; if you go around behaving like a moose in rut, you would disrupt traffic on a freeway, not to mention birds in a forest glade.

Wear what you like. Don't worry, be comfortable. But getting comfortable, considering the ghastly weather most bird-watching is done

---

* A Canadian wouldn't have wanted to belong to any club that would accept Groucho Marx as a member, or anybody else for that matter.

in, is no cinch. Here are some, if not surefire, at least well-worn suggestions:

It is better to be drier than not. So far, the best thing for keeping dry is Gore-Tex. There may be other materials as good—certainly there are others that claim to be as good—but it is a wise birder who doubts all such claims until otherwise persuaded. Yes, rubber coats and trousers will keep the deluge off your backside, so will plastic laminated ponchos and so forth. But they will create a deluge on the *inside*. In all but the coldest weather, with any but the slightest exertion, you will quickly be as wet from sweat and accumulated moisture inside the rubberized and plasticized gear as you would be if you ran naked in the storm. With Gore-Tex, this doesn't happen so much. On the other hand, anything with a Gore-Tex* lining costs about a billion times as much as any comparable garment without it.

Another thing about Gore-Tex is that it deteriorates rather rapidly. This year's new Gore-Tex jacket might not be as waterproof at all next year. But this is not a permanent deterioration (whether manufacturers mention this little wrinkle in the literature they stick all over the garment is a good question; mostly, they don't). To maintain its waterproof ways, Gore-Tex has to be washed frequently. Washed in *hot* water in an automatic washing machine. Dried at *high* temperature in an automatic dryer. Sometimes, it even helps to *iron* it after that. This seems so contrary to every natural response we have to space-age textiles that it sounds stupid, but it works reasonably well and is the only way that serious outdoors people will get their money's worth out of Gore-Tex stuff and not be left feeling like they've been had.

Layers, of course. You want to wear lots of layers of things for two reasons:

1. Between every layer is a layer of air, and air is the best insulation of all. Unless, of course, it is the only insulation. Then it is worse than nothing.

2. You are never warm enough or cool enough for long. The weather changes. Your exertion changes. With layers, you can add a little, or

---

* *Disclaimer*: The author has no financial interest in Gore-Tex or any of its licensed merchandisers, sadly.

remove a little, and it is no big deal. If all you are wearing is a buffalo robe over skivvies, you don't have a lot of room to maneuver.

New space-age materials (polypropylsomething-or-other) "wick" moisture away from your bare flesh and spread it among the outer layers of clothing. How it keeps these wet outer layers from "wicking" back through to your bare skin is something I don't entirely understand.

Anyway, a whole bunch of thinnish layers will be a whole lot lighter than a couple of bulky layers, and you will be able to move your arms with reasonable ease. Also your legs.

A note on socks: If things are going to get wet, the only kind of sensible socks are wool. There is something about latent heat that has to do with wool that I studied in high school physics (or chemistry) that is probably extremely relevant right here. Even wet wool socks will keep your feet warm; miraculous, but true.

Boots are another item you can blow your financial brains out on. Something to remember: You will almost never be carrying a heavy pack at the actual time you are bird-watching. Therefore, there is no need to wear hiking boots that weigh ten pounds each. Go lightweight. On reasonable trails in dry weather, sneakers are fine.

On reasonable trails in even slightly damp weather, though, your feet won't be happy feet unless they are dry. There are lots of lightweight, Gore-Tex-lined hiking boots around to choose from. They cost the earth. There are also lots of good waterproofing compounds for boots without Gore-Tex lining. A lot of these compounds work better if, after you goop them on, you blast them with a hair dryer so the goop soaks in. Your new boots won't look so pretty after this kind of treatment, but your tootsies will thank you for it.

Hats: Finding a toque or a woolly watch cap that has been tucked away in the bottom of a jacket pocket can sometimes be the loveliest discovery of all. Stick one in there and forget about it. As for the rest of your hat needs, what you want in a hat is something that is waterproof, provides a good sun visor, has plenty of ventilation, is snug enough that it won't blow off in a hurricane, is loose enough that it doesn't cut off circulation to your brain and that doesn't make you look even dorkier than you already do, dressed the way you are. There is no such hat.

Truly fastidious individuals are going to enjoy bird-watching about the way truly fastidious individuals enjoy sex: their minds will be on something other than the main attraction. Plunging after a good bird often means mixing it up with whatever is around by way of mire and bramble, and if this is off-putting, the only alternative is slide presentations by renowned birders at evening lectures in church basements.

Why Watch Birds?

There isn't a whole lot else to choose from.

I mean, when you get right down to it.

You can watch people, but you have to keep your observations superficial, you have to remain aloof, otherwise you—when it comes to taking in some vital intimate detail or other—will end up becoming one of those people neighborhood parents warn their children about.

You can watch flowers. Flowers come in nearly infinite variety, so do bugs. It has been conservatively estimated that if all the bugs were to die at once, we would be up to our yingyang in dead bugs. The only thing flowers have going for them is that they don't scamper away and hide after you get a glimpse of their stamens or whatnot. And I don't want this to come as a shock to any confirmed lepidopterists, but even butterflies are bugs. A big deal is made about monarch butterflies migrating all the way to Mexico. But after that, where are you?

You can watch squirrels. Raccoons. Mountain goats. Alligators. You can watch anything the hell you want, but there usually isn't that much of it that stirs the mind within a reasonable jaunt. A single moose, or a bear, along the highway through a national park will create a traffic jam a mile long, but what you are left with is a moose, or a bear.

A few other benefits the feathered friends offer:

Birds aren't all that furtive. A few are shy, but most feel reasonably comfortable in human company (for all they know, we're an elk or two). This means that you can watch them pretty thoroughly. Some you will never catch more than a flash of, but there are hundreds of them that, if you can get to where they hang out, will live free and easy right before your eyes. They don't keep much secret. This is an extravagantly generous thing for nature to have provided. If you want to know about endocrine systems, you will have to do some homework, but apart from that, you can become as expert as anybody else just by hanging around and keeping your eyes peeled. There aren't many other ventures where that is the case.

Few creatures—few anything—are as beautiful. If you like elegant understatement, there is the female Gadwall. If you incline more toward glorious overstatement, the Pileated Woodpecker or the Great Kiskadee. Come upon a Purple Finch in full breeding fettle against the dawn light and it can leave you weak at the knees. There are aesthetic rocks to be got off here. From tiny—a kinglet giving you an intimate peek at his ruby crown—to KABOOM!—a fishing flock of White Pelicans shimmering into focus in your telescope, like coming upon a fleet of battleships done up for a party.

They offer mysteries galore. A great many birds change their outfits and change them again. Figuring them out once is no guarantee you'll see anything slightly familiar the next time you look. And there are challenges beyond that. Which peep sandpiper is which? Not to mention the kingbirds that make their home in the Old West. Even in the books, they are hard to tell apart. In the Old West itself, they hardly ever sit still. They are the stuff of which madness is made.

And you can get a lot of return cheap. You don't have to travel far to get a seething sense of what is up with nature in your part of the world. You don't have to go beyond your own backyard. You don't have to spend a lot of dough on equipment. You don't have to join anything. You don't have to hang around with anybody else. And there are lots of good, useful authorities in print and on cassettes and CDs to help you along. If you go somewhere on vacation and the weather is crummy, as long as you've got your trusty bird glasses, the appropriate field guide and some rain gear, you can squish along happily, finding all sorts of things to compensate for the cabana bar being under eight feet of floodwater.

And not to get too philosophical, but *birds lead very ordered lives.* The circumstances in which they lead them are under fierce pressure and are often subject to drastic change, but still birds try to do what they have tried to do for hundreds of thousands of years. We, on the other hand, lead lives that feel as if they're coming apart at every seam and fraying along every edge. For us, there is some comfort in watching the progress of birds through their seasons. Things seem pretty straightforward in their world: hatch, grow up, get laid, raise a family. Step out of line and you're dinner.

Part 2

Bird Behavior

Sure, some of it is cute, but a lot of it is extremely disgusting, as you'll discover when you read about it in relentlessly graphic detail ❧ They might be birds, but they're real animals

Baby Birds

Once word gets around that you are a recognized authority on birds, people ask how come they never see any baby birds around.* They ask this because they are under a misapprehension. They look around and see little people on the way to becoming grown-up people. And they have seen fuzzy little Easter chicks. They have seen ducklings swimming along behind Mama by the lakeshore. So how come they never see any little Blue Jays or pigeons around?

It is a terrific question to be asked because it gives you a chance to throw around the words "altricial" and "precocial," exactly the sort of thing people think birders do, and exactly the sort of thing that makes them think birders are dorks.

Baby birds come in two varieties: the duckling, Easter-chick variety that can stroll around and pretty much feed themselves from the minute they crack out of the egg—and the other kind. The other kind, which are extremely ugly, are more like human offspring fresh from the womb: utterly helpless. Actually, they are often like the offspring of dogs and cats: utterly helpless and blind. "Naked as a jaybird" entered the vocabu-

---

* Every now and then someone will show up at your door clutching a baby bird that has fallen out of a nest, or been half-eaten by a cat, or both. The thing to do is make like you don't speak English. If they are neighbors and know you speak English, what you do is grab your chest, gasp "Call 911!" and collapse on the floor. By the time the subject of the bird comes up again the problem will have resolved itself, one way or the other.

lary* because new-hatched jays are entirely barenaked. Except for owls and hawks and herons, which are covered with down, these sorts of birds tend to be born naked.

Those barenaked, helpless-type babies, and they include all the songbirds, are altricial.† The other kind—ducks, geese, Easter chicks, killdeers, and so on—are precocial. Think of "precocious." It is as if human children arrived asking to borrow the car. Almost the first thing

* "Then . . . just as this stinkin' scapegrace was sliding down into his final sleep, a *babe* appeared in the heavens, naked as a jaybird and glowing like a red-hot ember. It came down and curled up next to him and kept him from freezing to death. *Natur*ally, Montanic says it was the baby Jesus."

—A report of Parson Montanic's conversion, from *Last Go Round*, by Ken Kesey, with Ken Babbs.

† A scientific term that likely means something.

Mama Wood Duck does is boot the babies out of the nest hole. Since this is sometimes twenty feet up, and nearly always over water, it quickly separates the serious would-be Wood Ducks from the dilettantes. It is not, however, an either-or proposition. While ducks and shorebirds are solidly at the precocial end, and passerines—the songbirds—at the altricial, in between you get, on a sliding scale of more of the one and less of the other and vice versa, grebes, rails, gulls, terns, hawks, herons, and so forth.

By the time a Blue Jay or a pigeon leaves the nest and enters society, it is as big as its parents and looks pretty much like them. If you look carefully, you can see some differences: juveniles tend to be colored differently from full adults; male kidlets are often marked more like females. They hang around their parents begging for food. They are so awkward that most of their landings could be listed under "pilot error." When juvenile hawks leave the nest, they are usually bigger than their parents, nature having concluded that being young and foolish and woefully inept, they will be no hell as hunters for the first little while and can use the extra fat to stay alive. Even at that, most of them don't.

Anyway, these are distinctions most people don't notice, so when they see two pigeons they assume they are just two pigeons, not that it might very well be a grown-up and a toddler.

You can live the rest of your life without ever having to use the words "altricial" and "precocial." If you find they keep coming up in conversation, you are in the kind of company about which people find it easy to say sarcastic things.

One enviable thing about the helpless little chicks of many songbirds is the fecal sac. It is as if nature had arranged for human infants' poop to come out in neatly sealed Baggies. In the interests of tidiness, all Mama and Papa have to do is drop these over the side of the nest.*

Bathing

Birds love baths. Migrating birds often don't care a damn for what you put out by way of food, but offer bathing facilities and they will stop to

* Or eat them. There is no avoiding information like this. It is always turning up.

wet their whistles and their whatnots. Birds that are around in winter *really* love baths. If you don't already have enough to do in your life, you can buy a little electric birdbath heater and keep the water melted. Be warned, though: one of the birds that stick around most places in winter is the European Starling. Starlings *adore* baths. If you keep nice warm bathwater in the backyard all winter, you could be buns deep in starlings.

The sound of water splashing into a birdbath from a slow drip can put birds into a bathing frenzy and lure them into your yard. The drip, from a hose hung in a tree or somesuch, has to be very slow, once a second, or even slower.

Bathing in water makes sense because (a) it is refreshing and (b) if you are a dirty bird, it will clean you up.

Some other common types of bathing aren't so easily explained:

Some birds like to thrash around in the dust. Thus restoring the bird's dirtiness, if I am not mistaken. See (b) above.

Some loll in the sun as blithely as vacationers at a Club Med, wings spread, tails fanned, shades, a novel by Judith Krantz.

The theory is that the dust might cut an excess of oil on the feathers, and something or other in the sun kills some of the bugs that make a comfortable living infesting birds.

That is also the theory behind anting. There are two styles of anting. A bird will splay itself across a busily traveled ant route and let the ants travel over and through its feathers. But sometimes a bird will pick an ant up with its beak and rub the insect over its feathers.* Some chemical ants exude is thought to relieve the heartache of bird-body parasites, although if you shop around, you can find the theory that birds just plain get off rubbing themselves with ants.

Begging

Don't confuse begging with the peremptory behavior of some jays and cardinals who have grown used to being fed at your feeder and, if it is empty, become demanding and rude. Sometimes, they will bang on your window until you do what they want. This isn't begging. This is terrorism.

Birds beg in two circumstances. In summer, young birds that are recently out of the nest hunker down and tremble and flutter all over and open their mouths and shriek, pathetically, "Feed me, feed me, *feed me!*" They follow their parents around doing this for days. Some of them get so excited they hop right on top of Mama to make their point. If they are fair-sized babies, such as Osprey chicks, their pathetic cries can be heard a long way off. They appear terribly spoiled, but they know what they're up to, squeaky-wheelwise: The chick that makes the most noise gets the most food. Whether this is an instinctive response by the parents to the begging cries, or they are simply trying to shut the little wretch up, is an open question.

In spring, adult females do almost exactly the same thing. Part of courtship among almost all birds is ritual feeding. Once the birds have paired up, the female goes all fluttery and helpless and puts on her childlike "Feed me, feed me!" act.

The male, if he is on his toes, feeds her something. Then wham! Into the sack.†

While it is absurd to see parallel behavior between birds and humans,

* This is hard on the ants, but who asked them?

† Science, in its quest to rid the world of the sort of valuable knowledge one gains in the street, is trying to retail the idea that courtship feeding is evolution's way of ensuring the female gets all the additional nutrition she needs in preparation for a time that is going to place great demands on her energy. This is what people mean when they say science sucks. A gift of food is a gift of love.

the ritual feeding of the female before getting it on goes back a long way—and I don't mean back to high school with fries and gravy. It goes back a *long* way. The loaf of bread, the jug of wine, and then the thou.

Boomers: Forget Boys Being Boys— Watch Out for the Girls

There are a few species of birds, none of which you run into every day, that have a method of getting it on that, if humans did it, would probably get us arrested. These are the Prairie Chickens, Greater and Lesser, the Sharp-tailed Grouse, and the Sage Grouse.

The females are drab, chickeny creatures.

The males, most of the year, are hardly any fancier. But when spring is in the air, they are transformed. All of them have air sacs—brightly colored fleshy balloons that are alluring to look at*—they can inflate, and lend a resonance to their lustful cries. The males, as if imagining they are discount-store peacocks, spread their wing feathers, fan their tails, cocking them for good measure, and stand around making booming, jug-band noises.†

So what happens is a bunch of prairie chickens or Sharp-tailed Grouse or whatever—a bunch of the guys, that is—get together on a regular piece of turf (the "arena," their booming ground, or courting ground, sometimes called a "lek," from the Swedish word meaning singles' bar) and inflate their whatnots and fluff themselves up and swan around looking vain and ridiculous. Now, in troop the females. They totter around among the puffed-up males and find one that suits their fancy, and give him the signal for "Let's go fool around" and off they go.

And they bang their brains out.

And then the female gives the male the heave-ho!

The next day, the males‡ set themselves out again and start puffing and

* Try to see it from their point of view.

† The Sage Grouse makes a noise like popcorn popping.

‡ Maybe 10 percent of the males do 75 percent of the shagging. Some guys just don't have what it takes.

booming.* And along come the females. The *same* females. And this time, they might select different guys and invite them back to their places. And again they bang their brains out. And *again* the female gives the male the heave-ho!

It is the same the next day.

And the next.

You know what we're into here? A pretty serious breakdown of traditional family values.

In the course of all this, because nobody has taken any precautions, the female gets knocked up. At which point, she stops going down to where the guys are hanging out. She builds a little nest and lays her little eggs and raises her little grouse or prairie chickens all by her little self. Single motherhood. She may never lay eyes on the father of her brood until next spring. And, anyway, if she did, how would she know he was the one?

Breeding Season

It is nothing you can set your watch by. Among migrant birds, courtship usually begins as soon as the females turn up. Sometimes, they arrive with the males; sometimes, as with Red-winged Blackbirds, they show up a week or two later. Birds that stay in roughly the same area all year round obviously depend on something besides a change of scenery to get in the mood. It can happen in the dead of winter. Crossbills will start to breed whenever and wherever they come across a big-enough stash of seed-filled cones. (Some African birds begin to breed as soon as it starts to rain. As long as the rainy season keeps coming around regularly, things go along fine, but a few years of drought can severely deplete the population.) Great Horned Owls begin their spooky love songs in February, often the coldest, wintriest month of the year, and always the longest. For most songbirds, it is April and May. For Arctic shorebirds, it may be June before the ice goes out. (They tend to trail the main migration north in the spring, since it is no use rushing to their breeding grounds, and they are usually the first birds back south, since there is no profit in hanging

* And popping.

around up there too long.) American Goldfinches often don't breed until August, sometimes September. They wait for the milkweed to produce its silky seed tufts, and for the thistledown, and use this to line their nests. Wood Storks won't do it if the water in the ponds where they forage for the slimy things they love to eat is too deep. Or if it is too shallow. Pigeons do it any time, and as often as they can. With Barn Owls, too, it is an anytime thing, but they are not as persistent as pigeons. Pigeons are in heat all year round, the same as us. This makes us freaks of nature, you, me, and the pigeon.

Brooding

A lot of songbirds nest twice—build a second nest after the first brood has checked out, lay a second set of eggs, raise a second set of kiddies—if everything is going well. If the weather isn't too extreme and there is enough to eat, some birds will do it three times: Mourning Doves are gluttons for punishment, and so are bluebirds and Song Sparrows, especially in the southern parts of their ranges, where the living is easy.

If nests are attacked by a predator early in the cycle, most birds rebuild nearby and have another run at it. If they happen to notice that a parasite bird, a cowbird, has laid its egg among theirs, some birds will rebuild elsewhere. Some rebuild *right on top of* the old nest, right on top of the old clutch of eggs. Yellow Warbler nests have been found with ten and twelve basements in them, each containing a big old cowbird egg.

Most birds don't start actually brooding the eggs—sitting on them—until the whole clutch has been laid, and for the most part, eggs are laid at a rate of one a day. Some birds chug them out faster, but laying an egg takes it out of you* and one a day puts a severe-enough strain on the apparatus. The reason they sit on them at all is because fertilized eggs can be stored for a long time with nothing developing if they are kept at a low-enough temperature. Things don't start cooking inside until a particular higher temperature is reached—when the temperature is below

---

* Try it and see.

34°C, give or take, everything is on hold—and to reach it, the bird sits on them and heats them up with its little body.

A problem is that bird feathers are famous for their insulating properties. This is why L. L. Bean dreamed up the down vest, and why evolution dreamed up the brood patch. The broody bird loses the feathers from its tummy in roughly the shape of a clutch of eggs. This bare patch has more than the usual number* of blood vessels near the surface, and these become engorged with blood. This hot little spot toasts eggs to perfection. If only the female broods the eggs, only the female develops a brood patch. If both parents brood, both do. In the case of phalaropes, only the male does, but the phalaropes are a different story altogether.

Cannibalism, Bird Barf, and Other Disturbing Matters

There are a lot of disgusting things about birds, even if you disregard the number of species for which vomiting is the preferred method of feeding the children. Vomiting is also a major means of self-defense with birds that eat a lot of fish. Grab hold of an injured Great Blue Heron—something you naturally only do because you want to take it down to the SPCA, where it can be saved—and it will vomit all over you. Take it into the SPCA and the people there will mutter, "Here comes some clown with a broken heron. It will vomit all over us." Some seabirds have a particular, special kind of oily, projectile vomit that sticks to you and won't wash off for days. And what about vultures? They poop on their feet to cool off.

Not all birds wait until their eggs are all laid before they start incubating. (I am not going off on a tangent. This will get disgusting again in no time.) Some birds of prey—eagles, for instance, and some owls—start brooding with the first egg out and may not lay their last egg for another couple of weeks. This means the children all hatch at different

* I don't know what the usual number is. I don't care.

times, and the first one hatched will be much bigger, and much hungrier, than the last one. So it eats it. The older brothers and sisters of the pelican family, and of storks and herons, will often eat their youngest sibling, usually while it is quite new to the world. If they don't eat it, they probably will trample it to death* anyway in their rush to be fed by their parents. Little pelicans have big feet and are not too careful where they put them. There is no sign that they show any remorse. There is no sign that their parents even notice.

Besides the species that eat their little brothers and sisters, there are some that push their little brothers and sisters out of the nest and let them die of exposure. Whooping Crane chicks do this, so do Sandhill Cranes. Not all of them do. Only the ones where the parents for some reason let the second chick survive. Usually, after the first one hatches, the parents peck the remaining egg to bits.

Gulls will often eat the chicks of neighboring gulls if the chicks are so foolish† as to wander away from their home nest. A gull chick that wanders away from its own nest is as likely as not to get eaten by its own parents if it happens to wander back home. So soon they forget.

Copulation

Birds do it. But how?

Clue: It isn't in the missionary position.

Something to bear in mind is that nearly all male birds are what is known as, in biological terminology, dickless wonders.

Apart from that, and given the alternatives, which, when you get right down to it, aren't many, it boils down to the customary approach among all other nonmissionary-oriented terrestrial mammals. The one known as—to use another biological term—doggy-style.

And accepting, as everyone readily will, that birds are neither mammals, nor entirely terrestrial . . .

They do it in the air?

---

* If you collect euphemisms, scientists refer to all this as "brood reduction."
† They can be pretty foolish.

No.

Birds have but one nether aperture through which everything passes; out, in; body waste eliminated, species propagated. It is called by many names, but mostly the "vent" or, more formally, the "cloaca." The object of mating birds is to press their vents together, that the sperm may flow, that the egg may be fertilized. In some quarters, this is referred to as the "cloacal kiss." They are quarters worth steering clear of.

But! There is an obstacle. The bird's tail. True, most species that choose the posterior mount by sheer instinct, and not because they are intentionally setting out to destroy the fabric of society, have to contend with a tail of some sort or other. A beaver, now there's an animal with a substantial tail. But it is here argued that a bird's tail is of another order of magnitude entirely. Even another kettle of fish. Neither as flexible as tails of other creatures, nor as pliable. It gets in the way.

The way they get around it—if you will pardon such a literal flourish—is this: She hunkers down. He hops on her back. He lowers his cloacal kisser in a searching, yearning sort of way. She, to get her tail out of the way, sort of swivels on to a haunch, so that they meet—and this is kind of interesting, now that I think about it*—as if they were doing it face-to-face in the biblically sanctioned manner.

* I won't think about it too much, or there will be talk.

In other words, what starts out doggy-style, ends up, thanks to the remarkable agility and flexibility of these fascinating creatures, being, in fact, the missionary position after all.

Holy gazonga! This makes birds the only other creatures, aside from us, that do it this way! At least generally speaking.

This is a scientific breakthrough. Bird-watching is one of the very few hard sciences where a layperson can still make valuable contributions.

Before we get on to orgasms, it should be pointed out that some birds have a penislike—what do you want to call it?—thing. A sort of protuberance. These are waterfowl: ducks and geese and swans. There is some thought that it serves as a sort of grappling device, what with the surfaces involved being wet and slippery most of the time. Now you'll want to know about orgasms. Do birds experience orgasms? Do they ever have multiple orgasms? Do they ever fake orgasm?

These are good questions.

Courtship

"The wren goes to 't."—Lear, *speaking of adultery*

At some stage, a practical decision has to be made: Who to boink? Or whom?

The females can shop around before deciding. Sometimes, they make a decision, but keep on shopping around anyway. For the males, it is mostly potluck.

Generally, the males pick out a territory and set themselves up in the business of defending it. They only defend it against their own kind. When a male of the same species shows up, the territorial male chases it away with warlike gestures. When a female of the same species shows up, he does the same—he doesn't notice any difference.* But if the female likes the cut of his particulars, she might decide to hang around. She goes soft and droopy and resists—''ignores'' is the better word—his efforts

---

* Not too quick on the uptake, wouldn't you say?

to get rid of her, and eventually a change comes over the male.* He starts coming on to her. It is the coming on that arouses our attention.

Some birds take on a new mate every breeding season: most of the songbirds do. Very few of them mate for life: the White-Breasted Nuthatch is one of the rare ones that do. Some mate—if you want to call it that—for a fast piece of ass: the so-called "lek" birds, the prairie chickens and grouse, but hummingbirds are the same. Slam, bam, and good-bye, although it isn't clear whether the male decides to hit the road or whether the female decides she doesn't want him around and shows him the door. And then there are those till death do them part: geese, swans, cranes, maybe eagles, that White-breasted Nuthatch, and ravens.

All right. At some point in all these species, the male and female reach a stage of mutual consent. They are going to do it. Now is when the major action starts, the foreplay. It ranges from fairly discreet to four-alarm, loop-the-loop insanity. Its purpose is simple: to get the hormones pumping, to bring them to a boil. There are as many techniques as there are species. More, in fact.

They fit vaguely into four categories:

1. Singing Your Heart Out
2. Wet 'n' Wild
3. Struttin' and Shakin'
4. Flying Circus

If there is a theme that runs through these, it is the male showing what a hunk he is: the toughest son of a bitch in the valley, the biggest, the best-looking (it is the only time of the year that the ruby crown of the Ruby-crowned Kinglet or of the Eastern Kingbird is much in evidence), a dead-eyed hunter, a good provider, a dynamite nest-builder (the male House Wren builds dummy nests; the House Wren that builds the most attracts the most mates; they like to have several).

Singing Your Heart Out might as well include the woodpeckers, although they don't sing. They are squawkers—but not in these circumstances. Instead, they drum. Each species of woodpecker drums to a

---

* It sort of sounds as if offering to beat the crap out of your beloved was great foreplay. Thank goodness civilization came between us and our animal selves.

different rhythm (fascinatin'; with practice, you can tell them apart—
new friends will start hanging on your every word once this skill is
revealed) and in mating season, the males look for something that makes a
big noise: a dead branch, a hollow log. The biggest and noisiest of them
all, the Pileated Woodpecker, likes a loose piece of tin on a roof or a loose
piece of siding, something that will reduce the folks inside to drooling
idiocy in a few hours. A few hours of drumming is nothing to a Pileated
Woodpecker. Inspired by love, it will go for days.

All birds make music as best they can when the romantic urge is on
them, and only a very few sing the rest of the time. The Northern
Cardinal is one of the rare birds that sing—as opposed to chirp or cheep
or bink or croak (the day-by-day conversation of most birds)—all year
round. In fact, the cardinal is one of the rare species in which both the
male and female sing. Most species leave it to the males, and most males
give up singing when the need to keep the family together and defend the
old homestead passes.

There are only a few birds that have song and not much else as their
whole seduction repertoire. Bobolinks, larks (the real ones; that is,
Horned, as opposed to the meadow varieties), and a bunch of the
buntings actually sing on the wing. The Bobolink holds his wings out
stiffly, fluttering them in a quivery way—it is a wonder he manages to
stay in the air—and makes trilling circles above the female, who is hiding
down there somewhere in the tall grass.

In *Wet 'n' Wild*, you find the tasteful understatement of the male Mallard,
who will turn his head and point, with his bill, at his speculum, you should
pardon the expression. The speculum is the flash of color in the wing that
looks vaguely like a racing stripe when it is folded. Or he will preen his kiss-
curly tail coverts. The Mallard has little kiss-curls for tail coverts, which are
the little top feathers on the tail. You also find the goofball Red-breasted
Mergansers, who undertake what look like drag races, stretching their
heads forward until their necks are parallel to the water surface and then
gunning their engines. Goldeneye males fluff up their head feathers until
they look like fuzzy baseballs and then rock back and forth, back and forth,
like rocking horses. And then there is the really showy stuff, the nuptial
dance of the Western Grebe. Cranked up on their feet, their necks in a
snaky S-shape, he and she whip back and forth like lunatic eggbeaters,
roiling the waters and getting into a state of advanced arousal.

Struttin' and Shakin'. At one end is the discreet and relatively low-key* dance of the horny House Sparrow. The tail is fanned and cocked just so, the wings droop. At the other extreme is the Whooping Crane, as is only fitting, the whooper being extreme in most things, whether it is its endangerment or its enormous size. Unfortunately, because they are such ungainly-looking creatures, this dance of theirs looks, to the human eye, boogaloo city. Bowings, stretchings, leapings, flappings, jumpings up and down. Think of a couple of National Basketball Association centers performing the Dance of the Sugar-Plum Fairies after they have smoked something that makes their eyeballs radioactive.

Flying Circus soars from the sensational to the sensational. Northern Harriers perform loops, figure eights, barrel rolls. Male eagles come swooping down as if to pounce upon the backs of their beloveds, who are flapping along, apparently all unaware. At the last moment before collision, she flips over on her back and they grab hold of each other's talons—like trapeze artists working without a net—and go somersaulting through the air. The Common Snipe is famous for coming booming down from a great height and . . . booming. He spreads his wings near the bottom of his dive and the sound—imagine a parachute popping open—makes a boom that causes the ladies to go round at the heels. More passionate still is the female American Woodcock after the male American Woodcock sits by his lonesome in the middle of a field going *Peent* in a melancholy way.†

Having tired of *peent*ing, the male takes off and flies in a spiral, everwidening, until he is a couple of hundred feet in the air. During this climb, he makes a whistling sound—it is the wind whistling through his wing feathers. Having reached altitude, he circles, warbling dreamily, and then *Dive! Dive!* Down he comes! Zigging and zagging like a mad thing! Until he plops down once more in the middle of his field.

And goes *Peent*.

This all, happening at dusk and often after (or in the predawn, when he

---

* They themselves believe they are getting down and funky.

† There is something melancholy-sounding about all birds that go *Peent*—the Common Nighthawk is another that does; perhaps, given all the possible sounds birds make, being stuck mainly with *peent* is depressing, and they've given up bothering to pretend otherwise.

will try his luck again), can be difficult to see and has to be taken pretty much for granted. But your ears will tell you something mighty odd is going on up there.

Crippled-Bird Act, Or Giving the Big Bad Wolf the Old Wazoo

The Killdeer is best known for this, but it ain't alone. Ducks do it. All kinds of birds do some version of it. If a predator approaches a warbler's nest, the warbler parent will start carrying on as if it had just come down with a bad case of the plague. It will pitch out of the nest and tumble helplessly to the ground. When the intruder whips down to eat it, the warbler flies away, going *Hee hee hee*. The crippled-bird act. The broken-wing act: approach a Killdeer's nest, or its chicks. The chicks freeze. Mama—or Papa, or both—flops at your feet, flops a wing awkwardly on the ground, and then goes flopping away, looking awkward and lame and easy to catch. Not easy at all. It stays just out of reach until it has lured you well away, and then it flies off, going *Hee hee hee*.

Sometimes you wonder. The sight of a hundred nesting Semipalmated Plovers on a stretch of Arctic shoreline, alarmed by your presence, each of them raising and lowering a wing in screwy unison, is probably only going to deter a very dumb fox.

The Purple Sandpiper has a routine attractively named the "rat run." When danger approaches, it hops out and lowers its wing tips to suggest hind legs, squoonches up its feathers to suggest a ratty hide, and beetles off through the grass, ratlike, squeaking piteously.

The broken-wing trick, of course, is only useful with a predator. With something entirely uninterested in Killdeers as a link in the food chain, like, say, a bulldozer, and inclined to roll over the nest quite uninten-tionally and squash it flat, the bird says the hell with it and flies—boom!—into the intruder's kisser. This is liable to make anything short of a bulldozer turn away. A moose, for example.

If you decide to put a bird through its defensive paces out of idle curiosity, remember that this places the poor thing under terrible stress.

Any stress based on the certain assumption that your children are about to become somebody else's lunch is terrible. So do it once to see if it really happens and, discovering that it does, screw off and leave them alone.

Eggs

Whole books are written that are field guides to eggs. Eggs are shaped the way they are for good and practical reasons that don't need to be gone into here.* The size of the egg tends to reflect the size of the bird that laid it. This makes sense. A hummingbird that laid a grade-A large egg like the ones you get at the supermarket would never lay another.† Egg-collecting used to be a respected pastime in and of itself. That was in the days when you would read that an ornithologist "collected" a bird. What he collected it with was a shotgun. This is no longer much admired. Neither is collecting eggs.

Some birds lay a whole bunch of eggs: a duck can turn out twelve or fifteen. Songbirds make do with a half-dozen or fewer. The farther north you go, the higher the average number of eggs laid, probably because evolution decided the chances of them hatching are slimmer. Even so, estimates are that with the average songbird, only about half the eggs end up as youngsters flying around, while in the so-called precocial species— ducks, geese, and so forth—it is only about a quarter.

Some otherwise respectable circles hold the idea that a fair bit of inter-egg communication goes on before hatching. Apparently, grumbling and clicking can be heard within, if you listen closely, and this is

---

* Nobody ever asks, Which came first, the duck or the egg? It is not an issue.

† Okay, here's one practical reason for the generally egg-shaped shape of eggs. Imagine you had an oviduct. Imagine an ovum was making its way through your oviduct, picking up a little bit of this, a little bit of that, to give it a hard shell and to give the shell its coloring. It takes most of the day, and when it got to the end, if it was shaped bluntly like, say, a cork, it would pop out, and the end of the oviduct would close with a slam. All this slamming would jar your brains loose.

interpreted as the babes synchronizing their watches* so they will all make their debut at the same time.

It was when the Peregrine Falcon's eggshells turned mushy that we realized how far DDT was being sucked up the food chain in our direction. Poets used to go on a lot about eggs. Symbol of hope. The future in its shell. The map of tomorrow in such an ancient shape.†

Ravens, crows, jays, skuas, and many different kinds of gulls raid nests and eat the eggs. That's not nice, is it?

Flight Patterns

The way a bird flaps its wings when it flies can be as distinctive as any physical mark. So can the way it belts along. Big birds flap their wings more slowly than little birds, so a dot flapping its wings slowly is a big bird a long way off, not a little bird closer by. A hawk-type bird that goes *flap-flap-flap-glide, flap-flap-flap-glide* will be an accipiter of some kind, a Sharp-shinned or Cooper's Hawk or a Northern Goshawk. But which? That is the tough question. A hawk-type bird that keeps up a steady flapping is none of the above. European Starlings are always in a big rush. The flight paths of woodpeckers and nuthatches are swooping up and swooping down, swooping up and swooping down. Life is a roller coaster. The explanation is that evolution decided that since these birds land on the sides of trees a lot, it would be easier for them if they could do it on the upstroke. That is a pretty good explanation except it doesn't explain the American Goldfinch, which undulates like crazy in normal times, and when it is horny really lets rip. U-u-u-u-p! And d-o-o-o-wn! U-u-u-u-p! And d-o-o-o-wn!‡ But you won't ever see any American Goldfinches landing up against the side of a tree.

---

* A figure of speech.

† Owls' eggs are round as Ping-Pong balls. So are kingfishers'.

‡ Energy efficiency might feature, though. A lot of these birds—watch a flicker; being bigger, it is easier to see—give a big flap or two at the bottom of their downswoop and then tuck their wings in tight as they rocket up and over the top, not so much gliding as traveling like an artillery shell: ballistically.

Some people really get into the way birds fly. In his book *The Private Lives of Garden Birds*, Calvin Simonds gives a breakdown of swallows, explaining precisely how each swallow species can be told from the others by whether it flaps and glides in circles, or in ellipses, or flaps up and glides down, or flaps but does not glide, or flies directly without a flutter, or flutters like a bat or . . .

Simonds goes on about this so much he sounds exactly like the sort of person you can meet birding with no trouble at all.

Here is what I know about swallows: The Barn Swallow is the only swallow in North America with the famous "swallowtail": its tail feathers stick back in a V. If you want to figure the others out by the way they fly, go ahead. You will be a big hit at parties.

You can tell a flying bird is a duck because it flaps so hard it looks as if it is about to have a heart attack. Ducks also have takeoff patterns. The so-called "marsh ducks"—Mallards, Gadwalls, teal, and the like—spring straight up into the air from the water's surface, Lord knows how they do it. Diving ducks need to race down the runway, and so do loons, swans, and geese. Watching a loon take off can make you think it's never going to. As for landings: the bigger birds stick out their webbed feet as if they were water skis and slide in. Oldsquaws don't seem to have got this right, yet. They end up facedown just about every time, arriving at the end of the landing spectrum that is called crashing.

Robins are about as easy to pick out as any bird around, unless they are flying overhead and you can't see their red breasts. Then they will fool you unless you notice the way they tuck their wings back at the end of each stroke, as if their wings are oars and they are rowing across the sky.

Blue Jays can be easy to spot even if you can't make out that they are blue, or jays, because a Blue Jay doesn't raise its wings above halfway; almost as if it were doing push-ups. Think of seals clapping.*

A couple of birds do odd things with their wings when they are not flying. The Northern Mockingbird flashes, you should pardon the expression, raising and spreading its wings to show off its white patches. It looks the way you look when you stretch your arms while yawning, the difference being that it doesn't yawn at the same time. The Upland

* Or don't. It's a free country.

Sandpiper gives a big stretch the minute it lands. If you see a bird do that the instant it lands, you see an Upland Sandpiper.

The only two species that appear to fly around just for the hell of it are pigeons and ravens. Pigeons, mind you, do a lot of things just for the hell of it, such as annoy you. You might think that, given the freedom of the sky, birds would do a lot of what amounts to getting behind the wheel and going for a spin. You would be wrong. Just pigeons and ravens. They appear to like it a lot.

The tips of owls' primary feathers are fluffy, allowing them to fly silently. Many people believe that when they swoop in and take prey, they have no need to make an extra effort to kill it. Pounced on without warning, it dies of fright.

One little matter needs clearing up. You sometimes hear that swifts flap one wing and then the other. If you hear that, say, "That is a load of bull" and walk away confident in your knowledge of avian behavior.

Formation flying: at least flying in V formation. The theory behind V-formation flying is that the bird in front thrashes up the air, creating more lift for the bird behind. According to the experts, there is more to it than just breaking the wind. Holding your open palm thumb up, fan your arm back and forth across the surface of some water. It creates little vertical whirlpools. The same thing happens in the air, but since wings flap up and down, these whirlpools are horizontal, and the trailing birds can, in effect, surf on them.

It gives rise to some interesting statistics. *The Audubon Society Encyclopedia of North American Birds* says: "In an analysis of bird flight formations, Lissaman and Schollenberger (1970) demonstrate that the power- or energy-saving V flight may give birds that use it 71 per cent more flight distance than the range attainable, say, by a lone bird . . ." I admire the hell out of that 71 percent. There is nothing wishy-washy about 71 percent.

Geese are famous for flying in Vs, but just because you see a V, don't go leaping to conclusions. Cranes do it, Great Blue Herons, swans, ibises. Sometimes, you will see gulls in a small V. The feeling is that birds any smaller than these don't get any benefit out of whatever it is that makes it work for the bigger birds.

As formations go, it is the only one that has a name. Nobody ever talks about the "blob" formation, or the "cloud-of-gnats" formation. This probably means something.

Flocks

Birds of a different feather flock together, too. So much for folk wisdom. In the fall, almost every type of blackbird you can imagine seems only too pleased to get into a big raggedy flock with every other type of blackbird—birds they wouldn't have been seen dead with in the summer—before heading south. When they get south, they often keep on sticking together, sometimes by the millions.

Small birds that winter in the North often hang out together. If you see Black-capped Chickadees in the snowy woods, look around for a White-breasted Nuthatch, a Downy Woodpecker, maybe even a Yellow-rumped Warbler. What do they have in common? More eyes make it easier to find food, many eyes can keep a better watch for predators. Depending on which theory you like, these small mixed flocks either disperse at night to avoid predators or huddle together to stay warm. I kind of prefer the latter, but then I am a romantic fool. Some ducks that raft in enormous numbers in the daytime will drift apart at night to make slimmer pickings.

Robins are big flockers in winter.

There is a lot of talk about how a lot of songbirds migrate higgledy-piggledy in huge, mixed flocks. As if they said to themselves, I think I will go and join a huge, mixed flock and migrate. Don't put too much stock in this. You might say subway commuters travel in huge, mixed flocks. On the other hand, you might say that big bunch of subway commuters is no more than a result of a whole bunch of people going in the same direction at the same time.

Hawks flock, at least Broad-winged Hawks do when they migrate. Sometimes by the thousands, but often way, way up there, so far up that to the naked eye, the flock resembles hardly more than a puff of dust on the sky. You have to look sharp. A flock of hawks, or of vultures, is called a "kettle." Watch a kettle of twenty or so vultures swirl along and you will understand why.

Lots of birds flock in migration that are otherwise pretty standoffish and independent once they get to their breeding grounds. Great Blue Herons, for one. Some go through profound personality changes when they gang up: the Bobolink is an eccentric, stay-at-home, mind-its-own business bird when it is north. At the end of the summer, it shakes off its

breeding duds, goes drab all over, and heads south in enormous flocks—
you would never know they were Bobolinks to look at them—to ravage,
in their thousands, the rice fields of South America. Down there,* they
call them "Ricebirds" and kill as many off as they can. Down there, they
are regarded as a menace.

Some flocks are weird to watch. House Sparrows will scrabble around
in a bunch on the ground and then . . . Boom! All fly up at the exact same
moment and perch in a tree or on a wire. There is no predicting when
they will do it, only that they will do it. Randomness that might throw a
predator's timing off. A long skein of starlings set on by a falcon will . . .
Boom! Coalesce in a second into a peppery, seething ball, that will make
an attacker think twice. A flock of Black Skimmers taking their ease on
the sand all point in exactly the same direction, as if they were a bunch of
weathervanes. They look ridiculous.

You can read† about the flock as "organism" and how each bird in it is
a molecule of the organism, not independent of it at all, scarcely existing
outside of it. This is the kind of stuff that engages the imaginations of
poets and moody philosophers of biology after they have seen a flock of
shorebirds blasting back and forth in tight formation, not one of them
zigging when the others zag, and always going flat out.

No one has ever come up with a solid explanation for why birds can do
this without turning into airborne bumper cars or going off in every
direction at once. That is why the game has been left to poets and
philosophers. Until now: Here is the reason birds can do this and you
can't.

Birds have little tiny brains. Their brains are so small that they can't
even think about feeding themselves, or getting laid, or looking out for
danger.‡ There isn't room in their noggins to do it. Instinct has to take

* Debating point: Are they our birds wintering in the South or are they their
birds breeding in the North? And who says birding isn't a lot of laughs.

† Not here, but you can.

‡ E. B. White: "How contagious hysteria and fear are! In my henhouse are two
or three jumpy hens, who, at the slightest disturbance, incite the whole flock to
sudden panic—to the great injury, nervous and sometimes physically, of the group.
This panic is transmitted with great rapidity; in fact, it is almost instantaneous, like
the wheeling of pigeons in the air, which seem all to turn and swoop together as
though controlled electrically by a remote fancier."

care of that stuff for them. What does that leave them to think about? Not much. Even in a little tiny brain, not much. So they can devote all their attention to formation flying. If you had that little to think about, you could pull off all the snappy maneuvers a sandpiper can with no trouble. With your great big brain, you would look like the Blue Angels by comparison.

Who says scientific theories are hard to come by?

Food: What Birds Eat

What *don't* birds eat is a more reasonable question.

Metal. That's about it.

A lot of them swallow stones to grind up food in their gizzards. Dinosaurs did the same thing. You don't often hear this connection between dinosaurs (the extinct ones) and birds (the only so-called living dinosaurs left). Until now. Did you think putting gravel in the bottom of the budgie's cage was like putting Kitty Litter out for the cat? Uh-uh.

Here, from the Audubon *Encyclopedia of North American Birds*, is what's on the Red-tailed Hawk's menu:

Field mice, house mice, rats, bats, grasshoppers, squirrels (red and gray), gophers, groundhogs, prairie dogs, cottontail rabbits, moles, shrews, chipmunks, muskrats, spermophiles,* weasels, skunks, porcupines, house cats, waterfowl, chickens, cattle egrets, gallinules, rails, pheasants, grouse, quail, doves, screech owls, kingfishers, woodpeckers, crows, starlings, grackles, meadowlarks, and any other small birds it can get hold of, ditto for snakes, including rattlesnakes and copperheads, turtles, toads, lizards, frogs, salamanders, crayfish, crickets, beetles, spiders, earthworms, carp, and catfish.

Say "Oog" if you like, but the entry on the Turkey Vulture's diet begins: "Eats almost entirely carrion, fresh to putrid . . ."

Birds that eat bugs and the like generally stick to bugs and the like, and

---

* Spermophile: a ground squirrel of some sort. From *spermophilus*, Greek for "lover of seeds." And good day to you, too.

birds that eat nuts and berries stick to nuts and berries, but the Tree Swallow, normally a bug-eater, can switch to a vegetarian diet when it arrives north in the spring, and a good thing it can, since it often arrives before the snow has gone and there isn't a bug to be found.

Black-capped Chickadees will take a sunflower seed from your hand without too much coaxing. Particularly daring White-breasted Nuthatches will, too.

Gray Jays can get powerfully chummy and will hop around your camp and take anything edible. The story has it that they will steal bacon out of the frying pan. I wonder about this, though. Edward Mustard is a magician who spent some years in the Far East, where he enchanted the locals with a routine he called the ''Peking Dancing Ducks.'' What Eddie had was a bunch of ducks standing on a flat surface. He would make some hocus-pocus gestures and, magically, the ducks would start to dance, lifting this foot, lifting that foot. Little did the audience—or the ducks, come to that—realize that the flat surface was a cleverly disguised electric griddle, and Eddie was turning up the heat.

I always think a bird that would land on a frying pan full of bacon must be a nitwitted bird. Unless the frying pan was cold. Considering what other birds will eat, I guess I wouldn't put eating cold bacon past a Gray Jay.

Pigeons produce a milk that is remarkably similar to the milk mammals produce and feed to their chilluns. The big difference is that both males and females turn the stuff out. Flamingos do the same. The method of transmission is different, of course. With birds, it is that old devil regurgitation.

Heating and Cooling

Let's get it said and get on with our lives. Turkey Vultures poop on their feet to cool off.

If you think about the thermodynamics of that, if "thermodynamics" is the word I am groping for, it would have to be one real hot Turkey Vulture that could be cooled off by pooping on its feet.

Wood Storks do the same thing. Other birds make do with panting. They open their little beaks and pant. It looks stupid, but it must beat pooping on your feet.

Different birds have different body temperatures, and these can go up and down 10°F depending on what the bird is doing. It drops when they go to sleep—or when it is cold outside. Hummingbirds use tremendous amounts of energy: this is one reason you hardly ever see them sitting around. They have to be eating all the time. Since they can't eat at night, being asleep, and since they have only a little space for storage in their crops, they lower their heart rates. Their body temperature drops along with it, into the high 60s F. They chill out. Sometimes, they go too far and turn into hummingbirdsicles. You can store live hummingbirds in the fridge, and thaw them out after. When they sleep, it is more as if they are hibernating.

To stay warm, birds fluff themselves up. It is where we got the idea of wearing a down coat. On hot days, they do the opposite, squishing their feathers down flat.

Don't their bare feet get cold in the wintertime?

No.

If it is really cold, they will fluff themselves up and sit down on their feet. Besides that, their feet have hardly any blood vessels in them, so there is nothing much to freeze up.

Some birds that spend more time than most standing around on snow and ice have feathers on their feet. Ptarmigans grow feathers on their toes in wintertime. Owls and other birds that pick stuff up with their tootsies have muscles on them, and have feathery insulation on their feet to protect them.

I guess this is the place to mention that in winter, the Ruffed Grouse's toes swell up and turn its feet into little snowshoes.

Homosexuality

The Birdwatcher's Companion puts it down to skewed sex ratios.

Pigeons seem to go in for it more than most, but pigeons go in for everything more than most.

Canada Geese. Yup. Maybe it has to do with so many of them giving up the rugged wilderness life and becoming city slickers.*

Sometimes with gulls, you will get a couple of females forming a happy bond and one of them laying fertile eggs as a result of some nimble male having breezed through before the females settled down in domestic harmony. You can bet that this serves to confirm them in their ways.

Gay tendencies are said to be especially notable among Western Gulls in California. This comes as a surprise?

Hunting Habits

The way a bird hunts for food can give you some clues about what kind of bird it is.

If a bird is hovering, it is most likely a hummingbird, a kestrel, a Rough-legged Hawk, a Ferruginous Hawk, a kingfisher, or some kind of tern. Some other species will hover in a pinch, but they don't make a habit of it.

If you see an egret in the shallows dancing its buns off and racing around like a lunatic, it is a Reddish Egret. Other wading birds wouldn't be caught dead doing this. Sometimes, it shrugs its wings back like an umbrella. Nobody is exactly sure why it hunts this way. There are theories: That it stirs up the stuff on the bottom. That its spread wings cast a shadow that cuts down on reflection. That the slimy little things it eats say to themselves, "This cockamamie bird is too loopy to worry about" and take inadequate precautions.

---

* Don't get me wrong. Some of my best friends admire the heck out of Canada Geese.

Brown Creepers start low on a tree trunk and tootle up. Nuthatches tootle up, down, any old way. So do Black-and-White Warblers.

Any bird that whips out of a tree, grabs a bug (sometimes you can hear its bill snap shut), and whips back is a flycatcher of some sort. Unless it is a redstart, a Canada Warbler, or a Wilson's Warbler, warblers with peculiar habits.

The Northern Harrier glides close to the ground, sometimes only a foot or two above it, its wings tilted up in a V. It is the only common hawk with that up-tilted V, which is called a "dihedral." When you see a hawk way up in the sky with it, it likely isn't a hawk at all but a Turkey Vulture. That Turkey Vulture glides wobbly.

Black Skimmers fly low above the water. Lowering their lower bill, they cut a long sliver of a furrow across the surface. When this lower bill touches a fish, it acts like a hair trigger. The top bill snaps down, the fish is snapped up, and the bird continues sailing along, not missing, as they say, a beat.

Ducks: Some dive, some dabble—picking daintily at the surface, or tilting their buns in the air as they browse on the bottom. The diving ducks will every now and then dabble. Once in a blue moon, a dabbler dives. But they don't make habits of it. And there are subdivisions: The American Wigeon seems constantly picking at the surface; the Mallard always seems to have its buns in the air. At some point, you are bound to read that deep trawls have hauled Oldsquaw up from two hundred feet down.

If a bird is hammering at a tree with its bill, it is most likely a woodpecker of some sort. This will hardly come as a surprise to you, except that nuthatches sometimes sound like woodpeckers. Don't let them throw you off. Nuthatches are indifferent peckers and don't have much going for them by way of rhythm. When pecking out the groceries, a Downy sounds a whole lot more rat-a-tat-tat than a Pileated. With a Pileated, what you hear is deliberate and heavy and a lot slower. Whack. (Pause.) Whack. (Pause.) Whack.

Sapsuckers drill a whole bunch of holes, sometimes rows and rows of them. These fill with, you guessed it, sap, that the bird, you guessed it again, sucks out. Except the second time, you guessed wrong. Sapsuckers have fuzzy-looking tips on their tongues; their tongues look almost like paintbrushes. They dip these into the sap and slurp it back. They should be called sapslurpers.

Imprinting

Imprinting is what happens when you take a look at something and get the idea stamped in your brain that whatever it is you are looking at is what you are, too. It probably takes place during the first few hours that a baby bird is out of the egg. Since the creature it most often sees in that period is Mama, it is nature's way of making sure species hang around with their own kind for the rest of their lives.

There are plenty of stories of ducks that have decided that they are human, or a human is a duck—this isn't entirely clear—and their mother to boot. Sometimes, they will do funny things as a result, like walking themselves to death following farmers who are plowing their fields with a tractor. They will imprint on the first big old thing that comes into view during those hours: a bus, a poodle. But if imprinting was given too much credit, there would be no more cowbirds. Until it packs its bags and moves out of the nest, the cowbird has seen nothing but its host parents, which might well be a pair of dinky little Yellow Warblers. When it comes time to get it on and propagate the species, you don't see cowbirds putting the moves on Yellow Warblers. They go after other cowbirds. There is probably less to imprinting than meets the eye.

Even if you have "Harley Davidson" tattooed on your bosom, it isn't entirely going to explain why your daughter climbed on the back of a hog behind a man named Filthy Louis and rode off.

Incubation

What happens to a human embryo inside its mother's tummy is what happens in the egg *outside* the tummy of a female bird. This makes it possible to share the job. Or, with the phalaropes, to turn it over to Daddy completely and blow this popstand. There are no flies on female phalaropes.

Generally, the drabber member of the pair does most, or all, of the incubating. It is definitely the case with the phalaropes, where the roles are reversed not only in terms of who sits on the eggs and raises the young, but in terms of who has the spiffier outfit. When the sexes look the same, they tend to share the task.

The purpose of incubation is simple: to cook the eggs at exactly the right temperature, a shade over 34°C, on average, to produce well-done young. At lower temperatures, the eggs are dormant; at higher, they are ruined.

Generally,* it takes longer to incubate a bigger egg. An albatross will spend more than eighty days hatching its eggs, while some songbirds get it done in as few as eleven. The Ruby-throated Hummingbird lays the smallest egg in North America, but has to brood it for about sixteen days because the female, who has been seduced and abandoned, has to spend so much time out of the nest feeding her little self.

Generally, the brood patches form on whichever sex sits on the eggs; if both do, both develop brood patches. In warm climates, birds may have to spend more of the day shading their eggs instead of sitting on them to keep them from getting too warm. This makes sense.

Incubating eggs is not a period of idle contemplation and bliss for birds the way pregnancy is for human females. Most birds are nervous and fidgety much of the time. The rest of the time they are run ragged. The eggs have to be turned regularly to keep them from getting overdone on one side. It is busy work. Generally, males continue to sing while the female incubates, and are defensive as anything when intruders show up. The male Rose-breasted Grosbeak is a lot flashier than the female and yet he sits on the eggs. More than that, he sings while he does it. If survival depended on not drawing attention to yourself, there would have been no more Rose-breasted Grosbeaks a long time ago. Sometimes, there's no accounting for what goes on.

Irruptions

It could just as well be spelled "eruptions," and it would be easier to understand. Every now and then, birds that normally don't migrate very far south go farther south than normal. When a whole lot of them do, then you have an irruption. The general thinking is that they do it because

* "Generally" is the best thing to remember about everything in birding.

their winter food supply crashes. Lemmings all rush into the ocean*
and—kaboom!—you've got Snowy Owls showing up all over the south-
ward landscape. Crossbills and Pine Siskins tend to move as far south as
they have to to find seeds.

If you are a beginning bird-watcher, it could be the first winter you
were on the prowl you were up to your patoot in Pine Siskins. And the
next winter, you didn't find a one. Naturally, you thought: (a) you were
going crazy, or (b) you had discovered a natural catastrophe. These are
the sorts of things that give bird-watchers lively evenings. Oh, well.
What you hit the first time was an irruption.

Life Span

Birds in captivity have an easy time of it compared with those on the
loose, and birds can live quite a long time in ideal circumstances. Few
wild birds encounter ideal circumstances. The average life expectancy of
all the little robins born next spring will be hardly more than a year. The
ones that live to adulthood might easily live on to the age of ten, but not
many make it to adulthood. Only a minority of songbirds do. You could,
if you wanted, calculate that of every hundred birds hatched, ten become
breeding adults.

Life can be even harsher for birds of prey. An adult hawk might live
until its mid-twenties. It might not, too, given the number of electricity
transmission lines it can fly into, and the engines of all those jets
crisscrossing the continent, waiting to turn it into slurry, and the number
of hunters ready to blast it to kingdom come. It does not take a lot of
brains to find a worm, and so even dumbish robins can pull through, but a
year-old hawk is a far more accomplished hunter than one on its own for
the first time. Among the difficulties hawks have to overcome is starving
to death through sheer ineptitude.

The rule of thumb is the bigger the bird, the longer it will live, all
things being equal, which, so far, they have never been.

* What? Lemmings don't all rush into the ocean? Get Research on the line. Tell
them I want to know what in hell is going on down there.

Migration

If there weren't mysteries of nature already, migration would be more than enough.

Some folks get pretty transcendental about it. The surging tide of life, the ebb. Affirmations of continuity.

Or you can just say that if some birds stay put after breeding they will starve to death when winter comes. So they bugger off. This confused the ancients. Aristotle was of the opinion that swallows dove into river mud and hibernated. It wasn't until the end of the 1800s that we figured out Aristotle, when it came to birds, didn't know dick.*

Some birds do fine hanging around. House Sparrows. Pigeons stick like glue. Grice.† Ruffed Grice grow snowshoes on their feet and get around just swell. Ptarmigans burrow into snowdrifts when the cold winds blow. The cardinal was once pretty much a southern bird. Then it worked its way north, and all the feeders we have put up keep it north when the snow flies.

With some birds it varies. Some starlings stay, some migrate.

With some species, it is a very big deal. The Arctic Tern migrates all the way from the very top, the Arctic Ocean, to the very bottom, the Antarctic Ocean, in the fall, and back in the spring. Commuting can take up most of a bird's life. The Eskimo Curlew, which may or may not be extinct, spends—or used to spend—nine months of a year traveling back and forth between the Arctic barrens and the tail end of South America. Talk about wearying.‡

For heroic journeying, nothing beats the Blackpoll Warbler, although the Ruby-throated Hummingbird is a popular favorite for blasting non-stop across the Caribbean. Such a thing was long thought impossible, and rumors got around that the Ruby-throats hitchhiked on the backs of geese and such. Don't believe a word of it. A Ruby-throated Hummingbird

---

* The Common Poorwill hibernates in cold weather, but what did Aristotle know of the Common Poorwill, unless maybe he took his March break in New Mexico? It wouldn't surprise me if he started the whole thing about sucking goats.

† Grice is not the plural of grouse, but it ought to be.

‡ If you had to do it, you'd give serious thought to becoming extinct, too.

wouldn't be caught dead hitchhiking. Here is a typical Blackpoll trip: Say it nested in Alaska. Time comes to leave, and it heads spang across the continent to the Atlantic coast, fetching up in Labrador, or Nova Scotia, or Maine. Here it takes a rest stop and loads up on berries. It puts away so many berries it about doubles in weight. Then off it goes. Voom! Some authorities say it flies nonstop for 85 hours. Some say 120 hours. I am no authority. All I know is that when Blackpolls finally touch down on continental South America, they are skin and bone, and out of breath.

Some birds have an instinct for it. Almost all the songbirds that migrate do it on their own the first time, and they either manage, or they don't. On the other hand, Whooping Crane kiddies go south with Mom and Dad in the fall, and back north with them the next spring. After that, they try to make it on their own, but it has taken quite a bit of schooling. Whooper chicks raised by foster parents don't show the slightest interest in migrating at all.

Some birds have Day-Timers in their heads. Cliff Swallows are famous for returning to the eaves of the old Spanish mission of San Juan Capistrano precisely on the Feast of St. Joseph—March 19. They have done it every year since the first mission building was erected in 1778, traveling to California from Argentina for the occasion. This is what they are famous for, but what they *actually* do is drift up in dribs and drabs like every other migrating bird. That is, in its own way, miraculous, but it's not A Miracle. It doesn't draw twenty thousand tourists, almost none of whom are raving bird-watchers.

On March 15, or the Sunday nearest, the folks in Hinckley, Ohio, celebrate Buzzard Sunday, marking the return of the Turkey Vultures to the cliffs where they breed thereabouts. Turkey Vultures are not buzzards. They are called "buzzards" in Western movies, but they are not, strictly speaking, buzzards. Buzzards are buteos, which are a type of hawk. But never mind. If celebrating the return of the Turkey Vultures is what the folks in Hinckley think of as a good time, they can call them whatever the hell they like.*

Birds' mental maps are often precise. Having the same robin return to the same yard year after year is not uncommon, but the entire population

---

* I hesitate to say that if you lived in Hinckley, Ohio, you'd be gratified if anything at all came back. At least they don't go around saying it is A Miracle.

of Kirtland's Warblers, after wintering in the Bahamas, returns to a section of central Michigan you could just about walk around in a day. Kirtland's Warblers are picky, picky, picky. They demand jack pines, but the jack pines must have grown *after* a forest fire, and they must only have grown *so far*—to somewhere between five and eighteen feet tall. Once a jack pine gets to be taller, a Kirtland's Warbler isn't interested in it as real estate. These jack pines have to be in a stand, and the stand has to cover an area of at least eighty acres. And since fires don't just happen all the time nowadays, and if one does somebody like as not puts it out, or tries to, and since jack pines don't stop growing, and . . . you get the picture?

No wonder there are hardly more than a thousand Kirtland's Warblers left. When you see Kirtland's Warblers, you want to say, "Try to be a little more adaptable, you dumb sons of bitches," but you might as well be talking to a rock.*

Migration lights up a bird-watcher's life because that's when something out of the usual run of neighborhood birds breezes through. The

---

* After all that, the Kirtland's Warbler nests on the ground.

rest of the time it is the same old gang. But don't think of it as—va-room!—north in spring, and—va-room!—south in fall. It is more like a year-round enterprise. Hardly a day passes when something isn't arriving or taking off or starting to get horny and making plans to head this way. Shorebirds bound for the high Arctic don't want to get there before the shore defrosts, so they're latecomers, and since it starts to ice up again about twenty minutes after they arrive, they're early leavers, too.

Some birds travel by night, some by day. There is logic to which do what. Eagles, hawks, vultures—birds that can surf along on warm updrafts and not have to waste a ton of energy flapping—naturally go by day. (These sorts of birds don't migrate over large bodies of water; not much there by way of updrafts.) Birds that can eat on the fly are day-trippers: swallows, swifts. But most of the songbirds, especially the ones that are easy pickings for predators, prefer night travel. Fly all night, find a place to eat, and hole up during the day. When the migration is at full boil, you can hear them tweetering and cheeping overhead in the dark sky. If there's a fullish moon, train your binoculars on it and watch them blip past.

When do they decide to move? There have been all kinds of experiments, and for a long time, the feeling was that it had to do with the amount of daylight. When the days grow short, it is time to light out. And when the days grow longer? Time to head back to the old breeding grounds. But what about birds that winter way down south in Argentina? And what about birds that winter around the *equator*, where the days are the same length all year long? Uh—wait! I know: there is always that old stirring in the loins.* Loins stir, take wing.

Anyway, you can see the problems with that theory. These days it is giving way to the idea that birds just have darned good calendars in their heads. Day-Timers as was written back yonder.

As for navigation, there is a theory that birds' brains contain trace amounts of metal and can detect changes in the earth's magnetic field, or there is magnetite in their gullets.† Built-in compasses, in other words.

---

* All the books make a big thing out of premigration restlessness. It is a feature of bird life, but you'll have to take my word for it. There are a lot of other things about migration I'm not going into either. A person can get bogged down in migration.

† Any theory about birds' brains containing something or other is interesting, since birds' brains are so small there is hardly even room in them for brains.

That's certainly a theory, and the scientific whizzes also incline toward it for ocean-run salmon and giant sea turtles that turn up back in the old hometown after years of traipsing Lord knows where.

Day-flying migrants get into less trouble when they can see the sun than when it's really cloudy, but since they can see into the ultraviolet part of the spectrum, they still have a pretty clear idea of where the sun is even when it is quite cloudy. Night-flying migrants seem to do better when they can see the stars. But there is no substitute for experience. Birds that have made the trip up and down the Atlantic coast a few times have a pretty good map in their heads, and a pretty good idea what the weather can bring. If a bad wind pipes up, it is time to head inland. This is news to first-timers and they are forever getting blown out to sea. Sometimes, they get blown all the way to Great Britain. A bird you wouldn't go out your back door to see can cause quite a stir in Great Britain if it lands up there.

In any case, birds have a whole bunch of different navigational tools and skills and use whatever is necessary to get along, same as you would if you knew your sextant from your azimuth. None of this, however, explains why these ace navigators persist in flying headlong into lit-up office towers in the night, knocking themselves senseless, and quite often killing themselves. There are lots of half-baked explanations (dazzled by the lights, etc.) that don't work when you think them through. It is a mystery within a mystery. Beware trying to solve every mystery in the bird world. Scientists are bound and determined that there is an answer for everything. They should give their brains a cold shower. Some things are mysteries and that's that.

If you feel deprived because you don't live near one of the so-called flyways, relax. Waterfowl and shorebirds prefer them, since they are mainly up and down the coasts and the Mississippi Valley—over water: this makes sense—but the feeling now is that most other birds ignore flyways and go wherever seems easiest and most direct.

Why do birds go wherever it is they go? Food is a big draw. Lots of ducks only go as far south as the first open water, but there is lots of water farther on and it is certainly warmer farther on. You would think the birds that go to Venezuela, say, could find accommodations nearer home. And there is some advantage to wintering closer to your breeding grounds, namely, that you get first dibs on good territory when you arrive back north. This would at least explain the tendency of juveniles to winter farther south than females, and females to go farther south than males. But Venezuela? Whatever, their patterns evolved long before the climate is what it is today—in some cases, before the continents were where they are today—and old habits die hard. The vast majority of northern species head for Central America. Since the vast majority of birds in the Western Hemisphere live in Central America already, it gets pretty crowded.

You can figure that whatever they do, and wherever they go, it must do them some good, otherwise evolution would have written it out of the script.

A postscript on robins as harbingers. Here's Edwin Way Teale: "For robins, spring arrives with the 35-degree isotherm. At that average temperature, frosts are out of the ground and earthworms are coming to the surface. The birds move north in the wake of spring thaws as the average temperature reaches 35 degrees." Things are different on the West Coast. "There is not any rise in temperature as far as the robin is concerned, during the entire two months it takes to migrate from southern states to treeline in northwestern Alaska. The average temperature is always 35 degrees." But, then, things are always different on the West Coast.

A postscript on the postscript. Any winter, you can find a couple of herds of robins mooching around in the snowy ravines near where I live (Toronto). These are mainly first-year males—bachelors, in other words—who don't give a damn for anything. When they get into the chokecherries, they get goofed up and leave purple splotches all over the snowdrifts.

Not another postscript at all: Birders in more northern latitudes get the blues in August, when there is too blinking much foliage to find anything to begin with, and most birds are busy with their molt and staying fairly still, deep in the greenery. This, though, is when to watch for a minimigration. When baby songbirds are big enough to look after themselves, they are often driven away from home by the adults* to

---

* You can hear sound biological arguments that there are not enough groceries on the local shelves to feed all these additional grown birds, and so somebody has to leave. My inclination, though, is to say enough is probably enough. Write if you get work.

venture off they know not where, and they know not why. They wander. Beginning with this "diaspora," as it is sometimes called, quite unlikely species can show up, often at feeders, in quite unlikely parts of the world, causing quite a commotion when word hits the hotline.

Mobbing

A good way to find owls: Listen for a bunch of crows going crazy. Rush to the spot. Look for what is driving them crazy. If they are flapping at, swooping at, shrieking at something, it is quite possibly an owl. Sometimes, it will be a hawk. Sometimes, it won't be anything at all. Crows sometimes just go bananas.

If there is an owl, or a hawk, what the crows are doing is mobbing it. Evolution concluded that if smaller birds can persuade predators to move on, the smaller birds and their children will have a better chance of still being alive the next morning. Mostly what they do is annoy the ass off the bigger bird, which, as often as not, is only trying to find a little peace and quiet.

Jays will do the same thing if there are no crows to do the job, and if there are no jays, little tiny birds will take their best shots. Little tiny birds—tiny as Blue-gray Gnatcatchers—will mob any threat near their nests: crows, jays, grackles. They will go through their repertoire of threat displays, but "displays" is the key word. They don't crash into the enemy except by accident, because at some visceral level, a lot of birds are more intelligent than we give them credit for.* On the other hand, cats don't understand the psychology of a bird's threat displays and so some birds get physical. Wander too near a colony of nesting terns and you will get your hair parted, and likely dumped upon into the bargain. Also puked upon. Wander near a nesting Great Horned Owl and you can get your scalp lifted.

For spectator appeal, nothing beats some great solo efforts. Often you'll see a hawk circling way up in the blue, and far below it a little bird flapping like a maniac, climbing, and climbing, and climbing, and climbing. It will be something like an Eastern Kingbird—a speck of dust taking on the Deathstar. It may need five minutes to get to altitude, but when it does, it starts dive-bombing the hawk's back, whacking it a sharp one on the head with each pass. Hawks complain like hell when this happens. Native North Americans called the Red-tailed Hawk "the talking hawk," and you'll understand why when you hear it start in about these sorts of injustices.

Molting

*"And when they're molting /
They're pretty revolting."*—Ogden Nash

Birds don't look the same all the time. There are other evolutionary reasons for this, but the main one is that it drives bird-watchers nuts. All kinds of things are confusing about birds, but "confusing" gets used in an official capacity with warblers in the fall. When they migrate south, and

---

* This is not to say chicken. Are chickens chicken? This is worth looking into. Watch for the sequel: *Downier & Dirtier Birding.*

while they're down there, many male warblers don't even vaguely resemble their flashy breeding selves. Neither do Bobolinks or tanagers. Put it down to molting.

A bird's feathers aren't like the hairs on your head—living, breathing things that keep on growing (if you're lucky). Once a feather has grown, it is dead, and the only way one that is broken or worn down can be replaced is for a whole new one to grow from scratch. Most songbirds molt all their feathers after they've finished with breeding, gradually, a bit at a time. Many birds molt a second time in the spring, but not completely, merely accessorizing the wardrobe to add sex appeal. A few birds change more often. When starlings go from speckled and relatively fancyish to their more customary unspeckled drab it is because the tips have worn off their feathers and is not a molt at all.

Birds molt gradually because growing new feathers takes an enormous amount of energy. Think what you'd have to go through to grow all your clothes. And, besides, if they lost all their feathers at once, they would be easy marks for predators, unable to fly away if they didn't shiver their brains out on a chilly night. Ducks, however,* lose all their flight feathers at once and can't fly a lick for a month or so. During this period, they go into something called "eclipse plumage"—the males looking as drab as the females—and try to stay out of sight. Waterfowl that live farther offshore—loons and grebes and the like—aren't so concerned about a formal eclipse plumage because there are nowhere near as many predators out there.

Because flight is so important to some birds, like eagles and vultures and cranes, they might take as long as three years to shed and replace a whole set of flight feathers.

Late-summer birding is a dull proposition because a lot of local birds are lying low while they molt. To get an idea of how ragged-assed they become, watch bigger birds like gulls and crows cruise overhead; the trailing edges of their wings have more holes than a hockey player's grin.

Also confusing are the names given to the various molts and the plumages that follow them. When is an adult an adult? When it gets full mature plumage (with gulls it can take as long as four years), or when it starts breeding (which it might do after a year or two, and often before it

* With ducks there is always a "however."

gets its full adult costume)? Mature plumage and breeding plumage are not the same thing, then, are they? With some species, things are more complicated still.

Puffins molt their fancy bills.

Nests

Item: There are actual field guides to birds' nests. If you decide to get one, you are becoming what sensible people think of as loose in the screw department.

Item: There actually is something called "bird's nest soup." It is made from actual birds' nests. You think that's gross? It isn't made from just any kind of birds' nests. It is made exclusively out of the nests of Oriental cave swifts—specifically, the Edible Nest Swiftlet. And Edible Nest Swiftlets make their nests exclusively out of Edible Nest Swiftlet spit.*

Item: There is an idea around that birds live in nests. That nests are their little homes.† Get it out of your head. Birds lay their eggs in nests and raise their young in them for a while, and that's it. Oh, a few birds roost in their nests, all right. Some owls and woodpeckers and the Cactus Wren take up residence in their nest holes, which are in trees, or cactuses. Male wrens often build a bunch of dummy nests to attract girls (the girls, after inspecting the male wrens' handiwork and giving the nod to a suitable builder, will usually then build their own nest just to be contrary). The male Long-billed Marsh Wren will often use one of the dummy nests he built to roost in, or at least to sulk.

Nests range from enormous (Bald Eagles' can weigh a couple of tons) to teentsy (you couldn't stick the tip of your index finger into a Ruby-throated Hummingbird's nest); from fancy (those high-fashion woven sacks that orioles go in for), to rudimentary (pigeons make do with a couple of sticks), to nothing at all (for Whip-poor-wills, a patch of ground in the forest; murres lay their eggs on rocky ledges and seem

---

* Now *that's* gross.

† It goes back even before Walt Disney and Hallmark cards.

perfectly satisfied). They can be found just about anywhere. Kingfishers and Bank Swallows excavate tunnels and nest at the end; Burrowing Owls use old gopher holes. Red-necked Grebes' nests are afloat. Ovenbirds build nests on the ground that look like little old-fashioned ovens. It is why they are called Ovenbirds.

For materials, anything goes. Hummingbirds use a lot of spiderwebs. Some birds add a little bird poop to their masonry; Cliff Swallows and Barn Swallows stick with mud. Some of the bigger flycatchers incorporate a snakeskin into their construction, the idea presumably being that the sight of it will make predators say, "Yikes! A snake! Let's get outta here!" With all the trash lying around nowadays, the flycatchers seem to be just as happy with a piece of plastic wrap as a snakeskin. Maybe they figure predators will say, "Yikes! Plastic wrap! Let's get outta here!"*

Eagles and Ospreys use the same nests year after year. Every year, they add a few more sticks to their nests. They do this until the nests get so big and heavy they fall down. Then they start building a new one. Some eagles will have a couple of nests in their territory; one year they use the one, the next year the other. This is their way of keeping bugs under control. You wouldn't believe the bugs that infest a bird's nest.

A robin's nest looks very much like every other robin's nest, and so it goes for every other species. Since most birds weren't around to see their parents build a nest (this isn't a joke;† sometimes when birds have two or three broods, the young from the earlier broods help build the next nests), they appear to be equipped with some kind of instinctive blueprint. Nevertheless, there are lessons to be learned: the first nests birds build are often pretty sloppy. Mostly nests are built by females. Sometimes, the males pitch in. Sometimes, the males collect the stuff and the females whip it into shape. But don't forget the phalaropes; the male builds the nest, the male sits on the eggs, the male raises the children. This can't be overemphasized in discussing equity.

Cowbirds only use other birds' nests and leave the other birds to handle everything else. Cowbirds are called "brood parasites." The Yellow-billed and Black-billed Cuckoo sometimes indulge in this sort of

---

* Nothing against Chaucer's Parliament of Fowls, but what's going on out there in the trees is hardly some kind of intellectual forum.

† I'll tell you when it's a joke.

irresponsibility, but nothing like the extent of the Old World Cuckoo, which does nothing but.

Eastern Bluebirds have had a hard time. They like to nest in holes, but so do House Sparrows and European Starlings, a couple of newcomers to North America who have tried to take over wherever they can, pushing the bluebirds out. These birds don't make their own holes and mainly have to depend on abandoned woodpecker holes. And there's the second story: The wooden fence post, going the way of horse and buggy,* has been replaced with metal posts into which not even the Terminator II woodpecker† can drill. So what you have is more birds competing for fewer holes. Take heart, though. Some devoted individuals have established bluebird trails—stretches of land where they have erected bluebird boxes, and the Eastern Bluebird is no longer in decline. (The same sort of thing has been done to keep the Wood Duck on the go.) Something to bear in mind is this: Little is made of the fact that bluebird boxes are just as attractive to starlings and House Sparrows—and to Tree Swallows—as woodpecker holes in fence posts. So how come the boxes aren't taken over, too? Answer: They are, but the bluebird-box-keepers go around and evict unwelcome tenants, sometimes nest, eggs, and all. Is this a mean thing to do?

During nest-building and brooding, birds are especially vulnerable. After all, their behavior becomes entirely predictable. This makes them especially nervous, and you won't do them any good by putting your nosy self into the picture. If you have a nest you can watch from a polite distance, you are lucky, but keep the distance or else you will screw up the works. Particularly unfortunate are the Piping Plovers that nest in scrapes in the beach sand just above the high-tide mark along the Atlantic coast. This has become the next best thing to the Indianapolis Speedway for morons with dune buggies and all-terrain vehicles. They are making the future bleak for the Piping Plover.

---

* Before long, people will say, "What is a horse and buggy?" If we're not careful, before long people will say, "What is a bird?" What will be around to say, "What is a people?" But enough of this philosophizing. Back to the game.

† Still on the drawing boards.

Pair Bonding: As Their World Turns

Mating for life is no big deal with birds, either. These do: swans, geese, cranes, albatrosses, Herring Gulls, Tufted Titmice, Cactus Wrens, White-breasted Nuthatches, Brown Creepers, and some crows. With the lek, or arena birds, it is a one-night stand. Male Ruby-throated Hummingbirds hang around for a few days of loving, but are gone before the nest gets built or the eggs laid. Most songbirds, herons, shorebirds, seabirds, and ducks stay together for a single breeding season, then start all over again the next year, when it's just as likely to be with somebody new.

Most birds, upward of 90 percent of them, are monogamous even if they are only together for a season, but for the ones that aren't, whew! Red-winged Blackbirds are as polygamous as anything. Why do females put up with joining a harem? Likely because the strongest male tends to have the best territory, and evidently it is better to have a good address and be one of many mates than to be the only beloved one in a poor part of town.

When it comes to cute birds, there is nothing cuter than the Black-capped Chickadee. So you wouldn't expect that the female is a raving sex maniac. Well, listen to this: after the pair bond is formed—you heard right: *after*—she trolls through the wildwood screwing every other male Black-Capped Chickadee she can find. This is going on *while* the nest is being built. It is a matter of nature imitating a country-and-western song.

In species where the female is inclined to wander, the male is presented with a challenge: he can either guard her around the clock, or he can bang her endlessly, never giving the poor female a moment's rest. Either alternative involves a lot of wear and tear on a fellow, and hardly leaves him enough time to eat, much less keep himself tidy.

Now, something everybody has seen, surely: a pair of romantic Mallards long after the family has been raised, Mama and Papa keeping constant company. Have you been sucked in, or what? So great is the competition for females that males pair up almost as soon as they complete their postbreeding eclipse molt. He earnestly keeps all other interested males at a distance through the winter, and through the spring, so that he, and he alone, fertilizes the coming eggs. Then, toodle-oo. He beats it the hell out of there, and shows no more interest in girls until, as before, his eclipse molt is finished and his hormones start to hum.

Piracy

The most insightful thing anybody ever said about gulls is that they don't hang around together because they're pals, but to see if some other gull drops something they can steal.* Anyway, nobody ever said life among the feathered friends was all sweetness and light. Magnificent Frigatebirds chase other birds until the other birds get so hysterical they barf up their dinners. The Magnificent Frigatebird hoovers it out of the air. (My advice is not to stop and think about this.) Black-billed Magpies and Scrub Jays sometimes gang up on other birds until they give up their food. Bald Eagles: O noble creature, unless you're an Osprey. If you're an Osprey, you're not even mildly surprised if a Bald Eagle comes along and bullies you until you drop your fish. A jaeger—just to show you how far this can go—a jaeger will *hold another bird under water* until, in desperation, the other bird just can't help but *vomit* up the entire contents of its stomach at which time the jaeger . . . Oh, never mind.

The technical term for these birds is "kleptoparasites." Isn't that a wonderful technical term? Feel free to use it.

Poop

Guano is bird poop found in quantities so enormous it can be mined. This is mostly done on islands off the east coast of Peru and the west coast of Africa. It is rich is phosphates and nitrates and makes good fertilizer. Chicken poop is the same, since it is about the only bird dropping found anywhere else in useful quantities.

Bird poop on your windshield is sometimes taken as a sign of good

---

* It is awful to think what the least insightful thing anybody ever said was.

luck. On the other hand, too much bird poop on your windshield, like, say, thirty-five tons, could be an indication of indifferent luck.

Elsewhere in this volume, you can read about vultures pooping on their feet.* Look for patches of white—it is referred to as "paint"—under trees, or splattered down tree trunks. Look up where it came from. See the bottom end of an owl up there?

Ms. Annie Graham of Ashton, Ontario, writes: Why is bird poop white?

Good question. Birds produce a different kind of urine than we do. *The Cambridge Encyclopedia of Ornithology* puts it succinctly: "Birds are uricotelic, which means that the nitrogen produced from protein metabolism is excreted as uric acid, as opposed to mammals which are ureotelic and excrete nitrogen as urea"—that comes out more a solid than a liquid. So solid, they require peristalsis to move this urine through their systems much as we require peristalsis to move feces through our systems (and unlike our urinary systems, where it moves along as a result of beer). Anyway, this comes out white. The little black flecks you find in it (if you look closely)† are the feces. The white stuff on your windshield is more accurately bird pee. From Canada Geese, you get green.

Preening

The four reasons feathers are so important to birds: (1) They make it possible for a bird to fly. (2) They provide insulation. (3) Without them, a bird would have a hard time getting identified by a birder. And (4) . . . Are you sure there are four reasons?

Feathers are not made out of miracle fibers. They are all natural materials, and as a result, they wear out. They break. They get tangled in things, and in each other. The get all smooshed up, the way your hair does when you sleep on it. Taking off with a primary feather twisted out of shape is like driving off with a flat tire.

That is why birds spend a lot of their spare time tidying themselves up.

* If you want to.
† Feel free.

Tucking feathers back into place, undoing tangles. It isn't just vanity. Birds have a little oil gland back by the part that, if they were turkeys, would be called the pope's nose. It is sort of a nipply dingus, and they spend a lot of time dabbing at it with their bills and spreading its secretions through their feathers. It is how swimming birds like ducks stay dry, and not just swimming birds. The quality of this oil varies from species to species, and two very watery birds, cormorants and Anhingas, produce a very low grade. If they're not careful, their feathers will get waterlogged and they will sink. To avoid this, they spend a lot of time standing around in strange postures—for example, on top of pilings with their wings spread and all their washing hung out on the line, as it were.

Preening also seems to be comforting. When birds are in a jam, even a get-down head-banging brawl, they will sometimes stop right in the middle of things and have a little preen before carrying on squawking.

Sleep

Let's get one thing straight. Birds do *not* tuck their little heads under their little wings when they sleep.

We'll get back to that in a minute—what they tuck where.

First, we should recall that by and large birds don't sleep in their nests.* Songbirds sleep *perched* on something. A branch, for instance. Now, there is this really nice theory. . . . But before getting into it, think about something for a minute. Think about the way *you* sleep. Most of the time, it is lying down. You could try doing it standing up, but face it, unless you were propped against something, the minute you conked out, you would fall down. So, there is this really nice theory that the reason perching birds, since they sleep standing up, don't fall down is that there are these things called ''flexons'' in their feet that when they go to sleep cause their toes to really *grip* on to the branch (if that is what they are perched on) and not let go. Sort of like a Vise-grip, if you know what a

---

* Unless they fall asleep while they're sitting on their eggs, or unless they're little baby birds, or unless . . . But we could pick nits like this all the livelong day. By and large, birds don't sleep in their goddamn nests.

Vise-grip is.* Anyway, there is kindly old evolution looking out for the little birds by creating a biological mechanism that keeps them from falling out of their trees when they slumber.

The thing about this theory is that there isn't a shred of evidence that it is true. For all we know, birds don't fall out of trees for the same reason you, for the most part, don't fall out of bed when you sleep, which, when you think about it, is a pretty good trick in itself.† Furthermore, it looks as if their flexor tendons are flexed whenever they perch on whatever they perch on, not just when they sleep, and who knows whether they're strong enough to keep a bird hung up there if for some reason it pitches over while dead to the world. So let's forget the whole thing, eh?

Woodpeckers and swifts sleep clinging to vertical surfaces. With Chimney Swifts, it is the inside of a chimney. Ducks and gulls and the like float. In the winter, ducks sleep in big mobs. Lots of birds roost in mobs after mating season: crows, herons. Some even nest in mobs—e.g., starlings under elevated expressways. Terns. Those little mixed flocks of woodland birds that band together in northern winters often sleep all piled together for warmth (or they don't, depending on which theory you like). What a bird wants most is a place that's out of the storm. Good places to look for owls in daytime are deep inside thick evergreens, hunched up against the trunk, or in clumps of wild grapevine. A tree full of roosting Wood Storks or Great Blue Herons is the living definition of ungainly, and goes to show you some creatures don't care how they look.

As for this tucking business, at the very most, some birds swivel their heads around and tuck their weary beaks under their scapulars, which are the feathers just on top of the shoulder. Think of it as pulling the quilt up over your nose.

* Sort of like I don't know what, otherwise.
† I would like to hear a theory about why that is. I bet it is a doozy.

Songs and Calls

Bird language is divided into two categories, songs and calls. There is another semicategory: body language. When a female wiggles her tush in front of a male, it has clear implications. Never mind. In this section, we are only concerned with songs and calls.

The Northern Cardinal has three basic songs. *Wet-year, wet-year, wet-wet-wet-year* is what one sounds like. Another goes something like *Bir-dy, bir-dy, bir-dy.* Then there's *Whoit, whoit, whoit.* They are whistled stridently. Sometimes, they are linked together, the one sliding into the other. Sometimes, it is just the one, or the other. Sometimes, they mix up a little medley. The cardinal is a good example for a couple of other reasons.* With cardinals, both male and female sing. Since a bird's song is the way it tells other birds of the same species that this is the singer's territory and to stay the hell away, in most cases, it is the male that does it. Not only do both cardinals sing, they are liable to sing all year round. Most birds only sing after they have staked out some territory and up till the kids have hatched. After the babies have flown the coop, there is a big silence in the bird world, one that makes bird-watchers wistful.†

If we may, for a moment, go back to *Wet-year* and *Whoit, whoit, whoit.* Phonetic versions of what a bird sounds like can be pretty silly. When you read about a towhee that sings *Drink your tea* and go into the woods listening for something singing *Drink your tea*, you will be bitterly disappointed. It doesn't sing *Drink your tea* at all. It shrills something that has sort of the rhythm of *Drink your tea*, and until you actually hear one singing it—a rare enough thing—or have somebody point out to you that what you are hearing is *Drink your tea*, you won't have a clue what is going on. It *sounds* more like *Wink-wo-tse-hee-hee-hee.* The Olive-sided Flycatcher sings *Quick-three-beers.*‡

Here is how Roger Tory Peterson describes the American Bittern's song: "a slow, deep *oong-ka' choonk, oong-ka' choonk, oong-ka' choonk.*" It

---

* It was clever of me to have picked the cardinal, wasn't it?

† That's their story. Actually it cheeses them off because it is harder to find birds when they (the birds) are keeping their mouths shut.

‡ It thinks it is singing *Drink your tea.*

can be difficult, sitting there with your trusty field guide, to imagine that sound live. It is far easier to do it the other way around. Get out in the marshes on a spring morning when the bitterns are horny, and when you hear a bizarre noise, work your way back to the bird in the guide. That way you will spend less time grinding away at books and more time bashing around out-of-doors. This is good.

There are tapes, records, CDs. Some of them follow their own prescriptive approach, some go page by page, bird by bird, through specific field guides. You can make yourself a lunatic trying to figure the songs out and remember them before you hear the actual bird sing. As with the printed guides, it is easier to hear something live and then go and figure it out. "So *that's* what that was," you will say, and feel proud as can be. Mind you, if all White-throated Sparrows sound the same to us, it is a different matter for other White-throated Sparrows. They can tell, from a safe distance, who is singing, and what territory is being defended.

Songs can be enormously frustrating. Hotshot birders do as well by ear as by sight.* Some of us have sat and watched, with our bare eyes, Blue-winged Warblers sing for hours at a time, and the next time we heard the

* That's what they tell us, anyway.

sound, we didn't have the foggiest idea what it was. "A bird of some kind" was the best we could come up with. "Probably. It doesn't sound like a bug."

The Ovenbird is famous for singing *Tea-cher, tea-cher, tea-cher!* So famous that people sometimes called it the Teacher Bird. A while ago, experts recorded an Ovenbird and ran it through a computer and discovered it doesn't sing *Teacher, teacher, teacher!* at all. It sings *Cher-tea, cher-tea, cher-tea!* The question is, since when you say the one or the other, they sound exactly the same to everything but, I guess, a computer and an Ovenbird, what difference does it make?*

Calls are pretty much all the public noises birds make when they're not singing. These they make all year round, and both sexes let fly. Roger Tory Peterson describes the cardinal's call thusly: "a short, thin *chip.*" This is so you can distinguish it easily from the call of the Chipping Sparrow, which he describes as "a dry *chip.*" It is this sort of thing that is sent to make beginning birders weep. Sometimes, it makes them so crazy that they say Shove it and take up playing the stock market instead.

The cardinal may have more things to say than that, but I don't care. That is more than enough to keep track of. Some birds have a lot more to say than they are given credit for. Robins say *Chirp.* They are about the only birds that actually do. Sometimes they say *Buk, buk, buk* like a chicken. A lot of birds make chirply little noises when they are migrating at night, which is when a lot of them travel. Presumably, this is to keep in touch with one another and to keep the old spirits up during the cold, dark journey. On dark nights, you can find birders staring up at a sky in which you can see absolutely nothing but maybe some stars. These hotshots will say, "Hear that chirply sound? That is a Hermit Thrush. And *that* one! That is a Ruby-crowned Kinglet." These people are hard to take.

Crows say *Caw* in one form or another, depending on what kind of crow they are. (Handy tip: The Fish Crow sounds as if it is cawing through a kazoo.) That's all you really need to know. But if you encounter crows coming on to each other, you will hear all sorts of other sounds—little warbles and coos and tweets and gurgles. This pillow talk doesn't get much mention in any of the books. Sometimes, crows make a loud rattly noise.

* That's something the experts have yet to answer.

Ernest Thompson Seton, who wrote a whole bunch of wonderful animal stories almost nobody has heard of anymore, made crows as articulate as the head of the average Western nation, with a vocabulary of maybe thirty words and phrases. These signified "All's well, come right along," "Be on your guard," "Danger," "Great danger—a gun," "Great danger! Wheel around! A gun, a gun—scatter for your lives," "Good day," and so forth. Well, who's to say?

The Northern Mockingbird is a case. It sings other birds' songs. One giveaway is that if you hear a Tufted Titmouse, for instance, singing at two in the morning, it is a mockingbird. Mockingbirds are the only North American birds* that sing at night. Sometimes, they go on for hours and make the neighbors cross. No one knows why mockingbirds sing other birds' songs. (Starlings sing other birds' songs, too, but not very well. Some British birds have begun mimicking the sounds of car burglar alarms.) It is one of the mysteries of nature. Do mockingbirds mock? That depends, I guess, on what you regard as mockery and how sensitive you are.

By my count, there are ten *Empidonax*† flycatchers. Some people claim to be able to identify them by sight. My position is this: I don't believe a word these people say. The key to identifying these things is their calls, although calling is not something they go in for much of the time:

Gray: *Chi-bit-seelp.*
Dusky: *Sillit-tsurrp-tselleet.*
Hammond's: *Sibit-tjurrup-tjelleet* (as if the Dusky had a frog in its throat).
Least: *Che-bek.*
Acadian: *Peet-see.*
Willow: *Fitz-bew.*
Alder: *Fee-bee-o.*
Yellow-bellied: *Chu-wee.*
Western: *Suwheet* (on the coast), *Whee-eeee* (inland).
Buff-breasted: *Pelik-sheew.*

You're welcome.

---

* Apart from goatsuckers. It goes without saying. What owls do is call.
† *Empidonax* is Latin for not being able to tell which freaking one is which.

Vomiting

Vomiting is often used as a means of defense by birds. Get too close to one, it pukes on you. The ones that go in for this are birds that live mainly on fish. You can guess how it smells. Some—they are known as tube-noses for other reasons entirely—manufacture a particularly wretched-smelling stomach oil that, being oily, won't wash off all that easily, and this is what they puke on you.* As if the contents of their stomach weren't bad enough to begin with.

Herons are defensive vomiters. So are vultures.

There is a famous local story about a flock of great big birds that got downed in an ice storm. They landed and got iced up even more, iced solid. A woman looked out her window and saw all these iced birds on her lawn and went out and carried them into the garage. Then she got the Humane Society on the line. The Humane Society came and loaded all the birds into their van like so many fire logs and took them down to the shelter. A couple of hours later, the local raptor repair depot got an urgent call. It was the Humane Society. "We got some really sick birds here!" the Humane Society said. "They are barfing all over everything, especially us."

What the raptor people, by careful deduction,† concluded was that the Humane Society shelter was full of Turkey Vultures. As they thawed out, these vultures took a dim view of their captors and started puking on them. It was nothing personal; it was instinctive. Far from being sick, it was proof that they were healthy as could be. It is something to bear in mind.

* Small birds are pretty much all fed regurgitated food. Think of a worm. Think of a worm regurgitated. There you have it.

† All things considered, Watson, I'll leave this one to you.

Walkers and Hoppers

You can get clues about species from the way the bird moves around on the ground.

Not all birds that run are Greater Roadrunners.

But just about the only bird that makes a habit of running a long distance or that seems to prefer chasing down its prey on foot is a roadrunner. They have been clocked at fifteen miles per hour. If you ran that fast, you would cover a mile in four minutes. Wild Turkeys can run faster.

Most songbirds—what bird-watchers call "passerines"—hop. Both feet at once.

Hop, hop, hop.*

But some walk. Left, right, left, right.

If you see a bird walking it is: a raven, a crow, a magpie. Jays do some of one and some of the other. Pipits are walkers. So are wagtails and starlings and meadowlarks. Most blackbirds walk, grackles and cowbirds included. There are four walking warblers: the Ovenbird, the waterthrushes—Northern and Louisiana, and the Connecticut.

Some waterfowl—namely, the ones like the loons that have their legs set away down at their tail ends—can barely stand up on dry land, much less sashay around.

* Somebody once said ducks can't fly, they are merely good jumpers. They may have meant it as a joke.

Part 3

Bird Parts

*All of them, including parts birds don't even know
they have* ❧ *Or if they do, they don't want to
admit it* ❧ *No wonder*

Banner Marks

Think of it as sort of a visual alarm. The outer tail feathers of the meadowlarks are white. So are the outer tail feathers of the Vesper Sparrow. Same with the Slate-colored Junco. The tips of robins' outer tail feathers are white. The flicker's rump is white. These are called "banner marks," or deflective coloration.

There are two theories. The first is that when a bird of prey is attacking one of these species and the intended groceries suddenly take wing, the sudden white flash will throw the predator off its stride (Hey! Whazzat?!) and it will miss its target, or strike a less vital portion thereof. This theory seems to be full of holes. If banner marks were such a good defense, why didn't evolution give them to more birds?

The second theory seems more sensible. When these birds take off, the flash they give—banner unfurled—is picked up by other birds, especially by other members of its own species. They realize trouble is on the prowl and they take care.

And it could just be they got marked this way because they got marked this way. I should've said there are three theories.

Bills

Bills go off in all directions. Flamingos have theirs on upside down.

When Darwin was in the Galápagos, he took one look at Darwin's finches* and said, "Evolution! This is going to open a can of worms."

Those finches all started off as the same bird, but each has evolved into a separate species with a different-shaped bill to fit it into a separate niche. The way they are counted at the moment, there are thirteen of them. As the niches change, and the surroundings, so do the bills. Evolution moves along hand over fist down there. The Woodpecker Finch uses a cactus spine to peck bugs out of bark; if its bill hasn't adapted entirely, it is at least on the right track.

If you persevere, you will someday be able to see the difference between a vireo's bill and a warbler's bill. The vireo's is generally a little thicker, and there is a little tiny hook at the tip of the upper bill. This is darned useful knowledge in a variety of social situations, such as if the conversation lags when a police officer pulls you over. The same with the difference between the bills on Downy (kind of wispy by comparison) and Hairy Woodpeckers. When anybody points these things out to you at first, though, you think they are nuts. Damned if you can see it.

The thing to think about regarding bills is that most birds don't use their feet for much except standing on. With birds of prey, it's a different story (also with shrikes), but most birds don't pick stuff up with their feet. And what would be hands if they were ours are what birds use as wings. So bills do most of the work. They are knives and forks, hairbrushes, fingers, weapons, nitpickers.

The snipe and woodcock, whose bills are so long they always appear as if they are about to overbalance, can open just the tippy-tips of those bills when they are probing with them beneath the ground and they snub up against a worm. Those flamingo bills operate sort of like the teeth of whales that strain plankton or whatever out of tons of seawater; their tongues are fringed and the sides of their bills slotted like sieves. It is the

---

* If it struck him as a remarkable coincidence that they were named after him, he never mentioned it.

same with shoveler ducks, which explains why they have never won a beauty contest.

When the question of love comes up, a lot of billing gets done along with the cooing. A number of species rattle their bills together to get their little hearts going pitty-pat. The bills of starlings and robins turn bright yellow in mating season.

Birdbrains

Zoologists rush to point out that, pound for pound, you won't find a bigger brain in any other creature except a mammal. On the other hand, most mammals don't have to fly by their own power, so maybe having a smaller, carry-on-size brain isn't so dumb after all.

This effort to keep weight to a minimum may explain the discovery that Black-capped Chickadees grow bigger brains in the fall,* adding a whole bunch of new cells in the hippocampus. The hippocampus seems to be the place where a lot of memory is stored, and in the fall, the chickadees need additional memory to keep track of inventory. In spring and summer, there are lots of insects to eat. As the weather gets colder, the insects disappear and the chickadees change their diet to seeds. They have to forage over a much larger area, and need to remember where seeds can be found. And they have to store seeds to make sure they have enough for the winter. And what good is storing seeds if you can't remember where you stored them? To make things more complicated, they need a whole bunch of different stashes in case one gets ripped off.

Once there is no more need to remember all this stuff, the additional brain cells die off and the chickadees direct their attentions to love, which is handled by instinct, same as with the rest of us.

* You either believe something like this, or you don't. It is like the designated hitter. You are either in favor of it, or you aren't. There is no middle ground.

Cloaca

The dirtiest part of the bird. The all-in-one hole. Procreation, evacuation. Efficient or what?

The cloacal sac certainly is. Produced by nestlings, it is as if your child manufactured its own Baggies and pooped in them. Very popular among a great many songbirds, and no wonder.

The cloacal kiss: bird boinking.

Colors

Evolution had good reason for giving birds the coloring they have, but for the most part, nobody knows what that reason is. Sometimes, it seems sort of obvious. Some birds can all but disappear against the background. This is usually called "cryptic" coloring and falls into the same category as that extremely butch camouflage gear that deer hunters wear so they will look like clumps of drunken scenery. These marks can be bold: Killdeer; or pretty subtle: woodcock.

As for the bright, even gaudy colors some other birds sport, at least part of the time, that's where nobody is quite sure what evolution's reasoning was. To be gaudy is as good a guess as any; to make the creature stick out. Then other birds will recognize it on its territory, either males and steer clear, or females and throng in to party. In species where the female alone sits on the eggs, she is usually the duller number.

Frankly, though, it all doesn't make a lot of sense. Why is so much coloration so higgledy-piggledy? Some species highly marked, some close relatives drab as can be. Between the Wood Duck and the Gadwall there could hardly be a greater gap in the costume department. At the same time, each is not one color or another with a little highlight here and there, as we humans are, for example. Each is marked in a dizzyingly intricate pattern that, if it is purposeful, is purposeful beyond anything imaginable.

When I said earlier evolution had a good reason, I'm not always so sure it's the case. Sometimes maybe evolution had no reason at all. Sometimes I think things just happened and got left that way. I can't see evolution putting a lot of thought into absolutely everything, and I'm satisfied that a lot of stuff around us that is mysterious is *absolutely* mysterious. That it has no explanation at all.

Color phases: Some birds go through obvious color phases that at least *appear* to have an evolutionary advantage. Ptarmigan and Snow Buntings are always keeping up with the seasons. If the bright colors of male goldfinches and many warblers are strictly sexual come-ons, there's no reason for them to stay in their party clothes when the party's over. And for male ducks to lose their Hollywood threads, when they shed all their flight feathers and are stuck vulnerably on the water, makes sense. (The summer and winter versions of the Oldsquaw are another case: both are quite glamorous, the winter version being almost a black-and-white photographic negative of the summer.) But, then, how about the permanent phases of the Snow Goose, some being blue and some not; so different that the blue goose was once thought to be a separate species entirely? There are the regular and dark phases of the Rough-legged Hawk. The white phase of the Great Blue Heron, confusing the hell out of everybody who is trying to figure out why this Great Egret is kind of weird. Those sorts of phase differences, called ''morphs,'' are akin to some folks being blonds and some being brunettes, and there is no evolutionary accounting for it.

Dimorphism

''Dimorphism''—the term—is used in two ways.

1. To indicate the difference in plumages between males and females.
2. To indicate the difference in *size* between males and females.

And not males being big and females smaller, the way they are in the movies.* The other way around. Females being great big hulking bozos† and males being tiny and kind of pert.

---

* Actually, Paul Newman is only five foot three, although you probably knew that. Robert Redford is five foot one. Richard Gere, five foot five. Humphry Bogart was four foot ten.

† Michelle Pfeiffer is six foot six.

Almost all female birds of prey are bigger than the male. Sometimes substantially. The male Cooper's Hawk and the female Sharp-shinned Hawk are pretty nearly the same size. This can make hawk-watching a real treat for the obsessive neurotic.

Why is another one of those questions. There is some logic in having juvenile birds of prey weigh more than Mommy and/or Daddy (depending on whether they're girls or boys) before leaving the nest. Novices are lousy hunters and so leave home with a few extra lunches packed around their waists to increase their odds of surviving, which aren't great anyway.

But the females being generally bigger? One suggestion is that the males are so aggressive in courtship that the females have to be able to duke it out with them until things calm down. Does that make sense to you? I hope not.

Ears

Two things off the top about ears and owls.

1. The ears that owls are named for—Short-eared Owl and Long-eared Owl—are not ears. They are feathery affectations, unlike the Great Horned Owl's horns, which are horns.* Birds' ears are on the side of the head, pretty much the same as yours. At least their earholes are. That external bit you are so fond of scratching and hanging earrings from, they do without.

2. The ears of owls are not the same shape, or in the same place, on each side of the head. One is higher than the other. The theory is that this gives the birds, which hunt creatures that scamper around on the ground at night, the ability to locate their prey by sound. Better stereo. Owls can pounce on little creatures burrowing deep down under snowbanks, presumably because their hearing lets them zero in on the spot. But don't go away with the idea that they can hear a whole lot better than we can, because they probably can't, at least not much.

* They are not.

The ears of American Woodcocks are actually in front of the eyes. This could be because their eyes are so big, evolution didn't have any other place to put them.*

Most songbirds— that is, what are called ''passerines''—sing in registers higher than the human voice, and as a result hear mainly sounds higher than the human voice. That's why they don't all fly away when even the yappiest bird-watchers yammer onto the scene.

Eyes

Birds' eyes are big. No matter what beady little thing you see peering at you, that is only the tip of the eyeball. Birds' eyeballs are sometimes the biggest things in their heads, including the brain. That sounds like

* It could have been an off-day at the drawing board. They tell you never to buy a car built on Monday or Friday. What they don't tell you is how to find out what day a car was built on.

something until you stop and think that they don't have much of a brain.

Birds' perception has to be quick because they have to be able to fly full tilt through a forest without bashing into branches. It has to be sharp because they have to be able to recognize a speck of food from a long way away, or pick out a speck in the sky that might turn out to be a hawk that has recognized them as lunch.

Hawks and eagles are famous for being sharp-sighted. Their eyeballs are better shaped for seeing distant objects than ours, being bulgier, and they have about five times as many of those little rod things in their eyes as we do. This led people to speculate that they can see five times as well as we can, but now the inclination is to think their vision isn't all that much better than ours at all. Except for owls, which can see about two and a half times as well as a human, and can definitely take in a whole lot more light. Owls' eyes are actually tubular, making them sort of like a pair of binoculars. Because of this shape, an owl's eyeballs can't move. Try this: Keep your head straight ahead. Roll your eyes up and you can see the ceiling; roll them down and you can see the floor; roll them left and right and you can see either side wall. An owl can't do that.

An owl makes up for this by turning its head, but an owl can't turn its head more than all the way around, no matter what you may have heard in school from that dingbat science teacher; otherwise, it would come unscrewed and fall off, like the cap of a beer bottle. An owl can't even turn its head *all* the way around. About three-quarters of the way is what it can manage, which isn't bad. Start off staring straight ahead, then swivel your head to the right; keep on swiveling to the right until you are looking over your *left* shoulder. Hurts, eh? An owl can also whip its head back around the other way so fast that you can barely detect it with the naked human eye. This is what made people think owls could turn their heads around and around in contravention of some basic laws of common sense.

Owls have eyes in the front of their heads, same as people, and as a result have considerable "binocular" vision, meaning 3-D. Hawks have quite a bit of binocular vision. Most other birds have very little, since their eyes are parked on the sides of their heads. That's why they cock their heads when they eyeball you. They often bob a little back and forth, the theory being that since they don't have 3-D vision and, as a result, no depth perception, they are taking a series of readings to figure out the exact distance you, or some morsels, are away. Watch a chicken checking out the scene. This might explain why the Spotted Sandpiper is such a lunatic bobber.

It appears as if some birds can see into the ultraviolet spectrum, something humans can do only after ingesting controlled substances. This allows birds to, among other things, keep a lock on the sun's location even when, to our eyes, it is invisible behind the clouds.

Pigeons' eyes are parked so wide that they as good as have eyes in the back of their heads. Woodcocks basically do. They can see straight up and straight back about as well as they can see straight ahead. If you want to take a woodcock by surprise, you have to tunnel in and come at it from below. Sounds like a lot of trouble. Skimmers' pupils are slit like a cat's.

Feathers

"Beautiful plumage."—*Monty Python*

Feathers are what make birds birds. No other creature has anything vaguely like them. Without feathers, birds would be God knows what. Grotesque lizards. They have distant lizardy relatives. If these relatives hadn't had scales, birds* might have turned out buck naked. Did you ever fondle a plucked chicken? Some of you may be able to imagine the patient curve of evolution, from scale, to bristly scale, to soft, fluffy scale, to feather. What we are dealing with here are the remnants of the earliest ancestors of the dinosaur, and there's no denying the pterodactyl and feathery *Archaeopteryx,* the Wright brothers of the bird world, are in the fossil record. But how they got from the one, to the others, to what we have flapping around now—*Archaeopteryx* had *teeth*—isn't all that obvious to me. And did the feathers show up to enhance the act of leaping off into the clear air, to carry the bird beyond the trees and into the broad sky, or did flight come along because the feathers had evolved and you might as well use them for something?

* Scales and feathers are constructed from the same building blocks of nature.

Unlike their scaly ancestors, birds are not feathered all over. That is, their bodies may appear to be feathered all over, but down at skin level, they are not uniformly* covered with feather follicles the way a (normally) haired-person's scalp is covered with hair follicles. Feathers grow in certain regions and along certain lines called "tracts," and between these can be bald spots. Birds possess some special talents. You might say something *made* your hair stand up, but you can't *make* your hair stand up. A bird has muscles running under its skin that can make its feathers stand up, and when it makes the feathers in their tracts stand up, it may well be letting the cool air reach the bare skin in between. Or, on a cold day, by plumping up its down to keep warm, a bird can double the puffery of its plumage. What are called "contour feathers" keep the bird generally, from the outside, discreetly clad, safe from sunburn, and streamlined as anything NASA has dreamed up.

Every type of feather, and there are a great many, has a special purpose, unlike, say, every type of hair on your body.† Some feathers are

---

* Penguins are, but if you see a penguin whilst jaunting on a normal North American bird jaunt, it is unlikely that this distinction will be the first thing that comes to your mind.

† Go ahead, tell me the purpose of the hair that grows in your ears.

even specialized beyond their specialization. Tail feathers, having particular work to perform, are not like other feathers. They are called "rectrices,"* and they are specialized to serve as the bird's rudder. But on woodpeckers, they have an additional job. Woodpeckers perch up against the sides of trees and peck the wood. Fine, except it is hard to take a real good peck if you are clinging to a vertical surface with just the toes of your two feet. This is where the woodpecker's tail comes into action as a prop: the woodpecker jams the tips of its tail feathers against the bark. Now, along with its two feet, it is supported by what amounts to a sturdy tripod. The woodpecker's tail feathers have a peculiar shape to permit this: no fuzzy tips, the feather's central shaft is stiffer and pointier and goes solidly to the end.

The flight feathers on the wings are officially called "remiges," but are otherwise and more familiarly known as the "primaries." These are the big, showy feathers that native North Americans like for their war bonnets. They are also what, in the days before personal computers, were sharpened and used as quill pens. Black feathers are tougher than white feathers and don't wear out so quickly, which is probably why evolution made the tips of the primaries of a great many gulls and the Wood Stork and the Whooping Crane and the American White Pelican black.†

Feathers hold their shape through an intricate bit of hook-and-latticework—barbs—that is easily visible through a magnifier, but you can get an idea of its effect by brushing a flight feather backward. It goes all screwy. Now run your hands the other way and see how crisply it flicks back into perfect shape. Some feathers don't do this; down feathers, for example, are just plain fluffy all the time. They trap air and keep the bird warm.

Another thing about feathers is that they are dead, unlike your hair or your fingernails. Cut your hair and your nails and they keep on growing. A feather that is broken has to be left to molt, or be pulled out, and grow again from scratch. If a hawk only gets a thrush's tail feathers, they start growing in right away.

Some other feathers are pretty much inexplicable: powder downs—

* From the Latin word meaning "They stick out of the pope's nose."
† Either that, or it was to confuse bird-watchers when they see them way the hell up in what amounts to orbit.

fluffy feathers whose tips are continually disintegrating into a powder that spreads through the bird's plumage; found mostly in hawks and herons. And rictal bristles—arranged around the mouths of many birds that catch bugs on the fly (flycatchers, nighthawks, and their kin, even American Redstarts)—are a bunch of short, almost mustachelike, bare feather shafts. Although swifts and swallows don't have any to speak of. Woodpeckers have whiskery feathers over their nostrils to keep from getting sawdust in their sneezers.

Feet

Birds' feet are just about as varied as their bills, cleverly adapted for each and every specialized situation, but who has time to go into all that? We will stick to the highlights.

For a long time, the thinking went this way: Birds that perched on branches and such to sleep* didn't fall off during the night. But a human being who went to sleep standing up would fall down. Obviously, birds had to have something up their sleeve, so to speak. This is where the flexor tendons run, and so everybody reasoned† that as the birds dozed off, these tendons flexed, causing the toes to close in a viselike grip on the perch. This explained everything and satisfied everybody, except it was wrong. At least it doesn't have anything to do with sleeping: these tendons are pulled tight over their heels, tightening the grip, whenever a bird perches.‡

Birds can walk around barefooted in winter without having their feet freeze right off. On especially cold days, some birds hunker down on their feet to keep them warm, and they also resort to a lot of one-foot standing, keeping the other tucked up. Some birds will go to great lengths to keep that foot tucked up and toasty, hopping around feeders for long stretches and even flying here and there without ever putting down the

---

* These are the passerines, or "perching birds," and do not include the Great Blue Heron, to name just one, which perches on branches to sleep.

† You probably would have, too. It was the in thing for quite a while.

‡ For my money, birds can just sleep standing up. That's all there is to it.

other landing gear. This naturally leads superficial observers to conclude that the bird has only one foot. Sometimes, this is the case, but hardly ever. However, this still doesn't explain why their feet almost never freeze off. It is because there is no muscle to speak of in the unfeathered part, only a few tendons, and, as a result, there are hardly any nerves or blood vessels. In other words, not much to freeze.

On the other hand, birds that eat with their feet—hawks and owls—and often as not kill things with them, have a considerable bit of muscle along the foot bones. And since these muscles need insulation, they tend to be the very birds that have feathery feet and legs. From a distance, this is what makes the Rough-legged Hawk's legs look rough.

"Palmate" is a word you hear. Actually, the word you hear is "semipalmate." It crops up in the names of a sandpiper and a plover. It means their toes are sort of webbed. As opposed to "palmate," meaning totally webbed, as in ducks. This semipalmatedness is baffling, since neither the sandpiper nor the plover that possess it spend any time swimming.* Not all swimming birds have webbed feet. On grebes and coots, the toes have big, floppy lobes† that work about as well.

The Ruffed Grouse grows its own snowshoes in winter; bony things that are like little ribs sticking out from its toes and that make it possible for the bird to walk on top of the snow. The Northern Jacana can walk around on lily pads because its long, spidery toes distribute its weight so much that it is, everywhere underfoot, as light as a feather. If the jacana were to stand on a single tiptoe on a lily pad, it would sink like a rock.

Genitals

Nothing much to see. A male bird keeps its balls in its belly, and they are nothing much to speak of either, most of the time. But when breeding season comes along, they swell up to as much as a thousand times the

---

* The only shorebirds that regularly swim are the phalaropes. The more you know about phalaropes the less surprising anything is. They sometimes spin around and around like eggbeaters, stirring up from the bottom the disgusting stuff they like to eat.

† Ditto those crazy phalaropes.

normal size. Can you imagine such a thing?* Think of the wear and tear on your shorts. The female does the same with her ovaries and whatnots.

The closest most male birds come to a hard-on is a big sploosh of sperm that is stored inside the cloaca ready to be ejaculated. This causes a considerable protrusion and is a sure sign that he is hot to trot.

The cloaca, of course, is the central doohickey in both sexes. *Webster's* defines it as "the common chamber into which the intestinal, urinary and generative canals discharge in birds, reptiles, amphibians and many fishes." The other definition *Webster's* gives is "sewer."

Male ducks and geese and swans, birds that firkle in the water, have penislike gizmos. But these are just stubby things they can use to get a grip in slippery circumstances. They are not the genuine article. If you are

---

* The reason it hurts so much when you get whacked in the nuts (excuse me; I mean to say why it hurts a male person so much to get whacked in the nuts) is that the nuts were originally an internal organ—as birds' are—that moved out-of-doors for reasons having to do with air conditioning and climate control, yet still retained many of the sensitivities of an internal organ. It would be like getting whacked in the pituitary gland or somesuch not originally built to take much whacking. At least that is one theory. If you find this comforts you at an appropriate moment, I am pleased to have been of service.

confused about Leda and the Swan, though, this should help explain things. Except, you know something? Gods that transformed themselves into creatures like swans, as Zeus did, had no trouble at all mixing and matching. For all we know, the swan that done Leda dirty had a full set of paraphernalia that was—how else can I put it?—godlike in magnitude. Leda, you will recall, laid a humongous egg from which Helen hatched.*

In other words, a hummingbird is hung like a hummingbird.

Gizzard (Also Crop)

If you have trouble seeing the connection between birds and dinosaurs, here is something that will knock your socks off. Both have (or one has, the other had) gizzards. A gizzard is part of the stomach, like a leather sack with a nubbly interior that grinds food to digestible size. The need for this becomes clear when you ask yourself the following question: How many teeth does a chicken have?

Some birds swallow little stones to help with the grinding in there. Dinosaurs swallowed bigger stones. These became rounded and smooth with time, and a pile of them leads dinosaur hunters to say, "Hey, we're on the right track."

Owls' gizzards separate the nasty bits—bones, claws, teeth, fur—from the tasty bits of their prey and bundle the trash into little furry pellets that the owl barfs up and that are very interesting to dissect if you enjoy that sort of thing.

Birds also have built-in storage, called "crops." They can fill up their crops, which are more or less the first stop down the hatch, with seeds or mice or whatever suits their fancy, and move to a more convenient, or safer, location to get on with the next dining stage. This can throw a bird's profile out of whack and give hawk-watchers, who sometimes have nothing but a tiny silhouette way up there to work with, the whim-whams.

---

* Quite a bit of this sort of thing went on in mythology. Gods were forever coming on as bulls. The girls seemed to like it, although they usually claimed later that they just thought it was a particularly chummy ungulate. Sure.

Meat

Meat is muscle.* The color of the meat varies in birds depending on how much the muscle is used. Turkeys—domestic turkeys—and chickens are basically flightless. Their breast muscles aren't much used to make their wings flap, and so their breast meat is white. They sometimes walk around, though, giving their leg muscles a workout, so their drumsticks and thighs are dark meat. Ducks—powerful fliers, powerful swimmers—are *all* dark meat. Pheasants (if you ever come on one under glass, look; you'll see) have white breast meat, as do grouse. This is because they are lousy fliers.

Nostrils

What can you say about nostrils? Most birds have nostrils, and those that don't—Anhingas, cormorants, and frigatebirds—start out nostriled, but give it up as they get older.

There are a number of seabirds—storm petrels, shearwaters, and albatrosses—that are collectively called "tubenoses" for the very good reason that their nostrils emerge from their noggins in the shape of a tube or tubes, like little wee sawed-off shotguns.

These tubular nostrils may be involved in the process of eliminating salt from these birds' systems, an important thing, since these birds only have saltwater to drink. Offer fresh water to a petrel and it won't touch it. These birds also vomit a particularly horrible stomach oil on anybody who messes with them. Then, again, all kinds of birds that get nothing to drink but saltwater don't have tubenoses. They appear to get rid of it through something along the lines of tears.

It isn't really clear how well birds can smell, but it looks as if birds that spend more time on the ground tend to be better equipped in the olfactory department than birds that mostly hang around in trees. Theories that vultures find their carrion by sight crash and burn when

* Unless it is gristle.

experimenters entice vultures to carrion by smell* alone. If it was up to me, I'd just as soon not find it by any means.

Skeleton

You can carry this sort of thing too far, but there are some handy analogies:

Wing. Take a look at your arm. Think of it as a chicken wing. If you were a chicken, the part of your wing we would eat that looks like a tiny drumstick is the part between your elbow and shoulder. The other part we'd eat, the one with those two bones that are joined at each end, runs from your wrist to your elbow. The tip of the wing is the skeletal equivalent of your hand, and if it doesn't look much like your hand, it is because there are only about three fingers and they are kind of welded together at the fingertips. There is even a thumb (it is drawn back like a hitchhiker's thumb, only more so; technically, it's called—pardon my language—the "bastard wing"). It probably helps provide a bit more lift.

Leg. A bird is standing on its tiptoes, unless that makes you think of a ballerina *en pointe.* That would be wrong. Think instead of a boxer on the balls of his feet. This is the case with lots of animals. Horses, on the other hand, stand on their tiptoe*nail.* Birds generally have four toes, one of which (what would be *your* big toe) points backward.† The reason it is so tricky for amateurs to draw horses and dogs and birds is because the hind legs (or, in the case of birds, their legs, plain and simple) have a backward bend that human legs don't. That backward bend is the equivalent of the human heel. The drumstick is the equivalent of the human calf, running from ankle to knee. The knee, when you figure out which part *is* the knee, bends the way a knee should, and everything becomes wonderfully clear.

---

* How do vultures smell? Awful. (A little bird-watching joke there.)

† Except—and you can go crazy excepting things, so I am trying to keep them to a minimum—except that some birds, most woodpeckers, for example, have two fore and two aft. Except for the woodpecker that has only three toes. The Osprey can move its rear toe forward if it feels like it.

Feel your breastbone. No, first feel your collarbones. In a bird, these collarbones are fused to become the wishbone. Now feel your breastbone. It isn't much of anything, almost concave. With birds, it is substantial, and with most of them, it possesses something even more substantial: a keel that sticks out very much like the keel on a sailboat,* which sticks down. This is something else that makes flight possible. Attached to this keel are four enormous—relatively speaking—flight muscles, two for pulling the wings down, and two for raising them on the upstroke. The keel-shaped sternum provides a lot of leverage.

With flightless birds the assumption is that they could fly once but evolved in the other direction,† kiwis and ostriches and so forth. One of the things that apparently evolved away was this keel. They are flat-chested.‡

It is as important to birds as to airlines to keep the weight down. Among bird tricks, one is to have a few hollow bones.§ Birds have a number of air sacs here and there in their innards, quite apart from the lungs. Air flowing through these seems to provide some internal air conditioning and, in swimming birds, some flotation. But in many birds, while they are in the egg, portions of these air sacs kind of seep into some major wing bones and thigh bones, and even into the head bone, creating hollow spaces that remain. If you think this sounds kind of weird, you still have a pretty good perspective on things. And where these hollowed-out bones remain most substantially are in some preeminent fliers such as eagles. The air sacs even continue in operation in their wing bones. The bird's bill could be another weight-saving device: think how much a mouthful of choppers would weigh by comparison.

Birds that need ballast as much as buoyancy, diving ducks and the like, don't bother with hollow bones. Here and there you find nifty adaptations: there is a kink in the necks of most herons that serves the same

* Called the "keel" or "sternum," which is from the Greek *sternon*, meaning "breastbone."

† If the implications aren't clear, these creatures evolved into flying creatures from flightless creatures. Then they evolved into flightless creatures from flying creatures. Where next?

‡ These birds are called "ratites," which is from the Latin for "raft," which is what their flat breastbones resemble to some. I can't see it.

§ Some land-bound dinosaurs had hollow bones.

purpose a spear-thrower's elbow serves when a spear is thrown. The spear in this analogy being the heron's long, razor-sharp bill. You probably guessed as much.

Skulls

Some sporting researchers thought there must be something to be learned from the woodpecker's skull. It has a lot of extra reinforcing in it so that the brain doesn't get scrambled the way yours would if you worked a jackhammer with your teeth. The walls of the skull are particularly thick, and the brain comes wrapped like a sausage.

The researchers thought something in the woodpecker's head bone might be usefully applied to improving the protective qualities of the helmets worn by motorcyclists and football players. Nothing seems to have come of this. It could be the funding dried up.

Syrinx: The Pipes—the Pipes Are Chirping

"Syrinx" is from the Greek for the kind of pipes the god Pan played. It is the bird's voice box. How poetic can you get?

Almost every description of how the syrinx works is terribly complicated. Except for this one.

When you pucker up and whistle, that is what a bird's syrinx does. Only instead of this being out where your lips are, it happens down in the bird's throat, roughly where your voice box is. How simple can you get?

The bronchial tubes rise up from the lungs—one from each—and, in most of the birds we see, they join together in the syrinx. As they enter the syrinx, they each pass through a washer-shaped* membrane. By cleverly tightening and loosening the muscles around these, or by increasing or slowing the amount of air passing through, the bird is able to make

* Or bagel-shaped.

sound, and to change it exactly the way you do when you're whistling. The better the singer, the more elaborate the arrangement of muscles around the syrinx, just as the better the whistler, the more nimble the pucker.

Since birds have two of these washer*-shaped things, some birds can sing two songs at once and mix them together. The Veery is famous for singing harmony with itself. Vultures aren't famous for singing at all. That's because they don't have any syrinx at all. They can croak fine, though. And grunt.

Tongues

One could go on a good deal about the tongues of birds.†

Some birds, cormorants and pelicans, have almost no tongue to speak of, since it would only get in the way when they swallowed great big fish.‡ At the other end of the scale are woodpeckers and hummingbirds, who have great big long tongues and steer clear of fish of all sizes. Woodpecker tongues are sharp and have rubbery sorts of spines toward the tip so they can get into holes and winkle out bugs and whatnot. These spines also glob up sap, which woodpeckers like, but not as much as sapsuckers. A sapsucker can't get enough of it. A sapsucker is a woodpecker that takes more sap in its diet, but it doesn't suck it at all. It slurps it up with a tongue that is fluffier, more like a paintbrush or a Q-tip than a regular woodpecker's tongue.

If that's all there was to woodpeckers' tongues, it would be cause for commotion, but what really brings the crowd to its feet is length. Woodpeckers in this hemisphere can stick out a tongue that's almost half as long as they are. Flickers can lick something five inches away. Not that

---

* Or bagel.

† One could write an opera about them. One could write an opera about any damned thing. Subject matter has never stopped opera writers. It hasn't even slowed them down.

‡ To prevent this from happening, the Chinese, who fish with cormorants, put an iron ring around the birds' necks. Then, the most they can swallow is little fish.

they do. Mostly, they tongue around in anthills, ants being high on the flicker's menu.

Woodpeckers can get this kind of length and control because of a strange connection the tongue has with the noggin. It is connected to something called a "hyoid apparatus,"* which—now get this—goes *down* the woodpecker's gullet, *out* the back of the base of its skull, *up* over its head bone, and *down* between its eyes, to where it is anchored, in the flicker's case, *inside* its nostril. You may find this unsettling because your tongue is not hooked to the inside of your nose. Or maybe there is some other reason. When the woodpecker sticks out its tongue, this arrangement works the same as if you had a trigger on your fishing rod that, when you pulled it, extended it another three or four sections.

As for hummingbirds. They also have real long tongues (they have the same sort of hyoid thingy as woodpeckers), but then they mostly have real long bills. The thing about birds with real long bills—e.g., Whimbrels, etc.—is that their tongues go right to the tip, and then some. Some hummingbirds have sort of brushy-tipped tongues for getting that good nectar,† and some have tubular tips—although the myth that these tubes extend the length of the tongues and the birds suck the juice up as if they had built-in drinking straws has been shot down. They just fill up these little tubes and haul them in and drain them. They can roll the sides of their tongue in to form a long, skinny trough, too.

This barely scratches the surface of birds' tongues, but life is short.

Wattles

Human wattles are wrinkly, flappy folds of skin under the chin, a condition, clinically known as "turkey neck," that is a boon to cosmetic surgeons. Birds take wattles in their stride. Some even go in for brightly colored ones to attract the opposite sex.‡ Turkeys, both domestic and

---

* So is yours, but it is small potatoes by comparison.

† Hummingbirds eat bugs, too. Not many people know that.

‡ You think you've got a handle on what attracts the opposite sex and then something like this comes along.

wild, are especially fond of them, and so are chickens. The bare heads of vultures can become quite wattlish in some species. Whether the bare flesh of some other birds—around the eyes in the pheasant, the eyebrows of the Spruce Grouse and Blue Grouse and some ptarmigans— constitutes true wattles is a subject for bitter debate among wattlophiles.

Whosis and Whatsis

Some bird parts crop up in the names of birds and can throw you for a loop.

Take, for instance, the Red-throated Loon, the Red-necked Grebe, and the Red-breasted Merganser. That should be straightforward: throat, neck, breast. Well, ha! The loon is red—and not fire-engine, either—in the Adam's-appley region, the grebe reddish from roughly the chin to the collarbone (if it had a collarbone), and the merganser, although why they decided to call it red is a good question, from about the bottom of the Adam's apple to the waterline.

With the belly, on the Yellow-bellied Sapsucker and the Red-bellied Woodpecker, they are referring to what we would think of as the chest and tummy. The robin's red breast becomes a white cummerbund at its lower belly. Plover bellies are a trial. In breeding plumage, the Black-bellied Plover has a black breast and a white lower belly, sort of like the robin. The Lesser Golden-Plover, on the other hand, has a black belly all over. Lest you think there is some consistency to this, the Rose-breasted Grosbeak's rose breast is flashy as can be, but hardly more than a bandanna at its throat.* By this measure, the Black-throated Sparrow should be the Black-breasted Sparrow.

Crests. The Crested Caracara's kind of sticks out the back. The crests of cardinals and Blue Jays and Pyrrhuloxias stick up like proper crests. The Tufted Titmouse should really be called the Crested Titmouse. The tuft of the other tufted creature, the Tufted Duck—a very occasional tourist—hangs down the back like a pigtail. Anybody who can distinguish

---

* Mind you, the grosbeak's beak is quite gros.

between the crestedness of the Great Crested Flycatcher and the capped-ness of the Dusky-capped Flycatcher deserves a prize. There is no uniformity among crests. The Scaled Quail has a dandy, stands up real perky. Some people maintain that the Lincoln's Sparrow has a crest, and that's how they know it is a Lincoln's Sparrow. Every time I see a sparrow that looks a little cresty, I announce, "There is a Lincoln's Sparrow."*

As for crowns, you can go your whole life, seeing thousands upon thousands of Ruby-crowned Kinglets and Orange-crowned Warblers, and never get a peek at their famous ruby and orange crowns. The Eastern Kingbird has the same kind of secret crown, but you'd never know it from its name. Another good question is why it is the White-crowned Sparrow when it could every bit as easily be the Black-crowned Sparrow, or the Black-and-White-crowned Sparrow. Or the Black-and-White-capped Sparrow. Or the Black-and-White-polled Sparrow. No one ever seems to mention its splendid gray breast. And belly.

Ears. Don't bother looking for the ears on the Short-eared Owl. They are too short to see. This is also sometimes the case with the horns on the Horned Lark, although there is no doubt about the ones on the Great Horned Owl.

Front. Greater White-fronted Goose. Golden-fronted Woodpecker. In bird lingo, the front is the forehead. But don't get the idea from this that the back is the back of the head. The back of the head of the Great Black-backed Gull is white. What is black is its back, like you'd expect.

Headed. There is the Common Black-headed Gull, which isn't all that common. It is just one of a bunch of gulls—six, I think—that are black-headed. Meaning their whole heads, as if they pulled stocking masks on and were sticking up the 7-Eleven. How this one got to be the official Black-headed one is another one of those good questions.† The thing is, they're all white-headed‡ except in breeding season. The Red-headed Woodpecker, on the other hand, gets redheaded and stays red-headed.

Neck. If the Ring-necked Duck has a ring on its neck, I'll eat a Ring-

---

* It is always a Savannah Sparrow.
† Especially since it is brown-headed.
‡ More or less. No need to get carried away.

necked Duck raw, ring neck and all. Where it has a ring, a white one, is around its bill. That's how you know it is a Ring-necked Duck. If you are determined to see a ring neck, go see the Ring-necked Pheasant.

Palmated. Or, at least, semipalmated. The plover. The sandpiper. It means their toes are webbed a little bit. Not all the way. Semi. You can't see this from where you're standing. The only woodpecker with three toes is the Three-toed Woodpecker.

Poll. The poll—as in poll tax, which has nothing to do with election polls or Gallup's either—is the head. And what is red, or black, as the case may be, with the Blackpoll Warbler and the redpoll is the *top* of the head. (For gulls with black heads, see *Headed*, above.) In the Blackpoll's case, black from the bill to the back of the neck. In the redpoll's, a round cap sitting above the eyes. Which is nothing like the black cap of the Black-capped Chickadee. That is more like the Blackpoll's. The redpoll's cap is more like the black cap of the American Goldfinch, which got left out of its name to make life easier all around. Come to think of it, Wilson's Warbler has a black cap of a similar sort, that gets downplayed, at least nominally. Actually, it is more like a yarmulke. The Blackpoll's black cap disappears after breeding season, by the way. So does the goldfinch's.

Ruffs. Every now and then a Ruff pops up here, blown in from Europe. It is hard to call because at the time of year the bird shows up, it almost never has a ruff. It is the same with the Ruffed Grouse. Most of the year ruffless.

Rump. It isn't around the bunghole, if that's the way your mind works. That part there is called the "undertail coverts." On the Gray Catbird, they are a lovely chestnut color. The rump is the lower back, just before the beginning of the tail. White-rumped Sandpiper. Yellow-rumped Warbler. The swallow with the yellow front and the orange rump is naturally called the Cliff Swallow.

Spectacles. As opposed to eye-rings. There is the Spectacled Eider, but there is no great fear of being trampled to death by them. Spectacles feature mostly among vireos, and would be eye-rings if they weren't joined over the nose by a little band, like a pair of eyeglasses.

Wings

The Wright brothers needed two things: one thing to give their contraption lift to get it into the air (and keep it there), while the second thing they needed had to make it move along. Wings and a propeller. If you look at a cross section of the wing of any bird that can fly, you'll see that evolution gave them all pretty much similar curves. The same sort of curve proved its worth at Kitty Hawk in 1903, and the aircraft wing hasn't evolved appreciably since.

If you don't already know about lift, here is a quickie. "Lift," in flying jargon, is opposite to the pull of gravity, which, when it gets out of hand, is called "crashing." Lift can be created if you take an object that is convex on the top and concave on the bottom (like the cross section of a bird's wing—what it would look like if you were looking at it end-on) and hold it in the wind. The wind goes over the top part faster—because it has to go farther—than under the bottom. This creates a vacuum on the top* and the curved thingy, the wing, rises into it: lift. Hold your hand out the window of the car flat and parallel to the ground. Now cup it a little. Amazing.

The difference in birds is that the wing is also the propeller, a combination that has never been successful in ordinary, wing-type airplanes (we'll get to helicopters later on). As a propeller, though, it doesn't work the way you probably think. Obviously, it doesn't spin around. Neither does it do anything else that's obvious: flapping straight up and down would get it nowhere, and rowing through the air isn't all that profitable because hauling the wings back to the start of the stroke would be a real, as the aeronautical engineers say, drag.

Instead, it works like this: remember that the wing is pretty much like your arm. Okay, now, the part from the elbow to the wrist is curved like the Wright brothers' (or a Boeing 747's) wing, and while it flaps up and down somewhat, it mostly serves as a standard fixed wing, providing lift.

It's the bit from the wrist to the fingertips—go ahead, call it the hand; we're all friends here—that provides the action. The finger bones are

---

* There are good reasons in physics for this, and if there weren't, your flight to Minneapolis would spend a lot more time nosediving than is healthy.

encased in skin and more or less joined together, but inside that skin, they are as deft as our fingers and hands. The long primary feathers sprout out of what pass for fingertips. These fingers can spread the feathers apart or squeeze them together until they overlap. They can roll them sideways so the feathers tilt upward, leaving slots in between like the teeth of a comb. Try that with *your* fingers. When they open these slots (look at the spread wing tips of a dawdling crow), they can fly really slow and not stall.*

This hand part is the really flappy part of the wing—the propeller. It pulls down with a big swoosh, digging through the air.† When it gets to the bottom, it ro-o-o-lllllllls its fingers and those long primary feathers sideways, so when they are pulled back to the top, they won't cause much resistance. (Try holding your hand out the car window, thumb up, palm forward, fingers together. Feel the air pushing it back. Now spread your fingers. Whoosh! All the difference in the world.) To cut the resistance even more on the upstroke, the fingertips/feather-tips make a little limp-wristed figure eight, kind of ducking forward.

To you, it still looks like plain old flapping. That's because you can't see all this happen with the barenaked eye. The wings flap too fast. Even the two flaps per second for the average duck is a blur; forget the fifteen or so a second in most songbirds, or the more than sixty every second for hummingbirds.

There is flapping, and then there are flaps. When an airplane takes off or comes in for a landing, the pilot lowers the flaps—wing extenders that slide out the back of the wing and curve down. This allows the aircraft to maintain lift at lower than normal speeds (thank goodness). Birds do much the same, lowering and spreading their tails as they land and take off.

Shapes. Birds' wings come in two general shapes, everything else being somewhere in between, or a combination of the two. One is long and skinny and pointy at the end, like a seagull's. The other is round and broad, like a Red-tailed Hawk's wing. Or a Broad-winged Hawk's wing, I guess you could say.

These are the two definitive gliding shapes.

If you look at the sails on modern sailboats, especially the monsters

---

* This has something to do with aerodynamics.

† A swimmer doing a butterfly or breaststroke wouldn't get far without hands attached to those arms. To belabor the obvious.

that race in the America's Cup, the mainsail, in silhouette, isn't shaped much different than a gull's wing; tall and skinny, sort of like a knife blade. The sails of old-fashioned ships, square-riggers, are more akin to hawks' wings. The long, skinny one lets gulls glide for miles *into* the wind, and it doesn't take much wind to keep them airborne, just as it doesn't take much wind to make a great big America's Cup yacht boom along *into* the wind, or almost. This kind of sail is actually a vertical wing, and the boats can sail into the wind because the curved sail is getting lift, same as a bird's wing.

Gulls can use these wings quite happily to soar up and up in lazy circles—they are the same shape as modern sailplane wings—but what they are ideally designed for is skimming over the wave tops. The all-time world champions at this are albatrosses, which are built like jumbo gulls; some of them have wingspans of eleven feet. They can fly for weeks without touching down, or without flapping.

The soaring hawks have wings built more like square-riggers, ships that were designed not so much to sail *into* the wind as to get blown along *by* it. But where these hawks want to get blown is not so much along as up. They want to get way up into the sky so they can spot little defenseless creatures they can pounce on and rip to bloody shreds and devour. So they look for thermals, rising columns of warm air, and get into these and let the rising air push them up. Also, it isn't a bad way to travel cross-country: get way up into the air and then glide down at a slight angle. It's how those modern sailplanes with the long, skinny wings travel long distances, taking the thermal elevator up and then gliding down to the base of the next one. Their pilots are always on the lookout for rising hawks, which are about as close as you can get to a signpost up there.

Other birds besides hawks soar like this, big birds especially: White Pelicans, Wood Storks.* Most other birds, especially the songbirds, if you watch them carefully, don't glide around all that much. A swoop here or there is about it, or when they are coming in for a landing. Meanwhile, even the accipiters, the hawks with the short, stubby wings that hunt in among the trees in the forest and have no call to soar most of

---

* In the southland, you want to watch that the little dinky thing soaring with the storks and the hawks isn't an Anhinga. Anhingas will do just about anything as long as it's unlikely.

the time, have gliding built into their normal wingbeat, which goes: *flap, flap, flap—glide; flap, flap, flap—glide.* Seriously. It's one way to recognize them.*

Hummingbirds and Helicopters. Some birds can hover. Hummingbirds hover best of all. They can hover forward, backward, up, down, just like little helicopters.

They can do this because unlike the other birds who mostly fly with what would be the equivalent of the human arm from the elbow down, as brilliantly described in the foregoing, all that the hummingbird has to speak of by way of wing is from the *wrist* down: that's roughly all that sticks out.

So its entire wing is as flexible as the *tips* of other birds' wings. This allows it to use its whole wing as a propeller, and to use the whole wing to make that clever little figure eight, whipping it back and forth. When a hummingbird wants to hover, it gets its body vertical—butt hanging down—and then flaps madly in such a way that its forward (only it would be upward in this instance) motion is exactly countered by its backward (what would be dropping-like-a-stone) motion, which results in its hanging magically in the air. It also has enormous chestal muscles, relative to its teeny size, so it can do this for quite some time.

Other birds that hover do it very much as the hummingbird does: let the body hang vertically, and flap forward—i.e., upward—at such a speed that they don't move. But their chestal muscles, even in big, tough birds like Rough-legged Hawks, are dinky in proportion to hummingbirds, and they can't do it for long.

All this flight stuff might sound nice to the daydreamer who imagines life among the clouds, but birds don't seem much inclined to fly for the

---

* In *Oklahoma*, you know how every night—*every night!*—that galoot and his honey lamb sit alone talking and watching that hawk make those famous lazy circles in the sky? Fine, except no hawks known to science, or even to me, behave in this manner. Nighthawks, which aren't real hawks, fly around at night, but they don't make anything anybody has ever confused with lazy circles. Neurotic circles, maybe. The hawks that are the lazy, circling kind don't do it much beyond late afternoon, because after that there are no thermals for them to ride—that is, to circle lazily on. My theory is, watching a hawk make lazy circles in the sky was the Wild West euphemism for submarine racing, and the whole song was designed to sneak dirty stuff onto the Broadway stage.

simple thrills it provides. Whenever birds don't need to fly—birds that live on islands where there are no predators and that don't have to catch flies for a living—it quickly evolves out of their résumés. This is what happened to the Great Auk. The only reason we say "deader than a Dodo"—which was also flightless—instead of "deader than a Great Auk" is because the Dodo beat it to extinction. Evolution, even in its wildest dreams, never imagined a predator like man.

Part 4

Deep Background

How it all began ❧ Where it's all likely to end ❧ Zen and whether, if you tether a lamb to your bird feeder, you're likely to find your backyard overrun with eagles

Archaeopteryx

"Archaeopteryx did not go to bed a reptile and wake up a bird."
—*Christopher Leahy,* The Birdwatcher's Companion

With *Archaeopteryx*, things have been up and down over the last 150 million years. In the last little while, it lost its ability to fly. This is a shame, since this happened only shortly after it took to the air. Mind you, it had been grounded not long before that, and this was a switch, because in 1861, when it was first discovered, it could fly like a bird.

If you saw an *Archaeopteryx* wandering around outside the house, you would think it looked like a weird chicken. We can go along with the crowd and agree that it was a bird, although it has some fairly reptilian* attributes. It looks as if our modern birds evolved from *Archaeopteryx*, or from some creature a lot like it. It would probably be wrong to say that *Archaeopteryx* and our birds descended directly from dinosaurs, though. It is more likely both birds *and* dinosaurs descended from the same sorts of reptiley things, called "thecodonts," of the type absolutely everybody knows as Pseudosuchia.† Birds and dinosaurs went on an evolution binge through the Jurassic Period (when *Archaeopteryx* made its debut) and the Cretaceous Period, after which the dinosaurs opted for careers as fossils.

---

* I mean that in the best possible sense, and not even slightly as a reflection on its character.

† Try ordering it the next time you're in a Japanese restaurant, but don't press the point.

By the end of the Cretaceous, there were lots of kinds of birds, all of them waterbirds and waders, including the spitting image of a flamingo. The two best-known that showed up between *Archaeopteryx* and this crowd that were definitely, positively, 100 percent birds were *Hesperornis* and *Ichthyornis*. *Hesperornis* was a gigantic loonlike flightless creature nearly five feet long. *Ichthyornis,* at eight or nine inches, was barely the size of a Least Tern, which it looked and acted very much like. Unlike the Least Tern, or any other bird today, *Hesperornis* and *Ichthyornis* had teeth. So did that weird-looking chicken that was wandering around in your yard twenty-five million years before these guys came along.

Besides teeth, the things you'd see that distinguished *Archaeopteryx* from a chicken were that it had a lizardy kisser instead of a bill, a long tail instead of a pope's nose, fingers sticking out of the bend in its wings— fingers with claws on them—and solid instead of hollow bones (although how you'd see that is beyond me).

What made it chickenlike were its feathers, its feet, and—particularly important to animals that have wings and want to fly—its wishbone (you would see that when you carved it for dinner), which is actually like our collarbones fused together and is among the things that make wing-flapping profitable as an exercise in getting from A to B.

If it flew at all, as its discoverers believed it did, it flew hardly better than a chicken, which is to say better than a brick, but not much. It flew, or at least glided—like a flying squirrel—along happily until the 1970s, when, boom! down it went. This was because new studies suggested that it stayed out of the air as much as you and I did before the Wright brothers. Its feet were adapted to *running* after its dinner, and its feathery wings weren't meant for flying at all, but evolved to trap prey, like great big hands, or a net, or a tent. As for the feathers, these could have evolved from scales that got worn all raggedy when the creature wearing them was thrashing through the brambles after food. The evolutionary value of feathers, especially to creatures that tear around as much as birds, is that you can regulate your temperature a lot better with them than with scales.

You know how it is with science. No sooner was this theory offered to a public dying to know the latest *Archaeopteryx* poop than another theory came along that said, Oh, yeah? What about the shapes of the primary feathers? In flightless birds, the quill goes up the *middle*. In birds that can fly, it goes up to one side: the side cutting into the wind. Think of where the mast goes on a sloop-rigged sailboat: at the front edge of the mainsail. Otherwise, it would be unstable and twist out of shape. These fossilized feathers were meant for flying, and there went *Archaeopteryx* into the wild blue. Okay?

Nope. This just in: a new theory that says the last one was full of holes. That when you look at the true business end of *Archaeopteryx*'s "flight" feathers, the quills aren't offset after all. Bringing it, splat! back to earth.

Feeding the Feathered Friends

Late every fall, a little flock of southbound Red-winged Blackbirds shows up at the feeder in my yard and makes itself at home for a week or so. They are males having a high old time with no females to distract them, or territory to defend. Eventually, one of them, sunnily disposed and cocky and comfortable, will holler *Konk-a-ree!*—the sound that, on the opposite side of the year, means any day now it will be spring. On the gray verge of winter, a sharp pang of longing; a bird's voice thrilling with the prospect of green, warm days and new life.

I go out and throw a rock at the son of a bitch.

That's a problem with feeders. They can be hard on the emotions. That's why the real trick is not getting the birds you want to come to your feeder, it is getting the birds you don't want to stay the hell away.

Feeders can be simple: a piece of wood left on the windowsill for woodpeckers. If you want bigger woodpeckers, put out a bigger piece of wood. Don't go overboard. You might get more woodpecker than you can handle.

Feeders can be somewhat more elaborate. I once designed this feeder: A bird lands on the end of a lever(A) that trips a hammer (B) that rings a bell (C) that wakens a Rottweiler (D) that sees a caged cat (E) and charges toward it on a treadmill (F), generating sufficient power to drive a series of gears and pulleys (G, H, I, J, K, L, M, N, O) that causes a spring-loaded Louisville Slugger (P) to whack a baseball (Q) through a pane of glass (R), triggering an alarm (S) that brings the fire department (T) on the double to chop down the front door (U), which breaks a thread (V) that allows the hands of a cuckoo clock (W) to tick forward one second to twelve o'clock, causing the cuckoo (X) to pop out and go "Cuckoo! Cuckoo!" twelve times, reminding you (Y) to toss a pork chop (Z) to the bird waiting hungrily at (A).

But I never got the right marketing. Marketing is everything these days.

Feeders can be expensive, or they can be quaint affairs constructed at home out of used plastic soft-drink bottles and empty cottage-cheese containers hung up with bits of string and coat-hanger wire. These look quite picturesque, especially if you have a rusting truck and a few old cars up on blocks around the place.

You can nail chunks of gristle to a tree if you like. Or a fish, if you want an Osprey to show up.

What other sorts of food should you set out? There are feed mixtures sold in supermarkets that look bright yellow because of all the cracked corn and hulled sunflower seeds they contain. This is the best stuff for attracting all the birds you wish would stay the hell away: pigeons, starlings, House Sparrows.

Nothing will keep House Sparrows and pigeons away. You can put out ball bearings and the bastards will eat them. But starlings can't eat most seeds that are still in the shell—their bills aren't strong enough to crack the shells open—so folks who feed birds prize sunflower seeds still in the shell over all else, especially the small, black sunflower seeds known as "small, black sunflower seeds."

There is no law against feeding starlings, but starlings are squabbly. They squabble mainly with one another, but five hundred starlings squabbling with each other on your feeder will discourage everything but other starlings, and pigeons.

There are all kinds of pigeon-proofing methods. None of them works, but there are so many of them that you will be dead long before you can try them all out.* Even if you find something that works, songbirds are disgustingly sloppy eaters. For every seed they swallow, they drop five on the ground. You think you can keep pigeons off the ground?

If you get serious about bird-feeding, you will be astonished to discover that squirrels have IQs of 170. As long as your IQ is higher, you will have no difficulty coming up with satisfactory methods of keeping squirrels out of your feeders.

---

* And much sooner, once you get your shorts in a knot.

House Sparrows? God knows. Even House Finches have gone ape in many places, hogging the feed and chasing other birds away.

Hummingbird feeders are easy to come by and the sugar solution to fill them is easy to make, and it is a treat to see how many bees you can attract, and ants. Suet is good for chickadees. Fresh orange slices appeal to orioles. I have heard of people putting out canned dog food for crows. I've always kind of wanted to tether out a lamb and see if I can pull down an eagle.

If you prefer plants that attract birds, most garden books contain a list of shrubberies guaranteed to do the trick at costs that are no more than phenomenal.

When to feed? Any season the spirit moves you. In snowy regions, most bird-feeding is done in the winter, but summer is fine and brings its own surprises. Some of the best birding on the continent is enormously enhanced by feeders. In decidedly nonsnowy South Texas, the winter tenants of the campgrounds in the Rio Grande Valley take bird-feeding seriously and make it possible for a day-tripper to fill a list in no time flat.

There is an old northern bird-feeders' tale that you shouldn't put out seed if you're going to disappear vacationward for part of the winter because the little dears you have suckered into dependency will starve to death when you cut off their supply and freeze into little bird cubes. This is not so. There is enough other food and often, these days, feeders around. Birds are pretty enterprising.

One thought for the yard-listing heavy breathers is that most of the so-called rarities that show up in the winter and late fall—the eastern birds way out West and the western birds Down East—show up at feeders.

Field Marks

One of the smartest things birds ever did was develop field marks. Before field marks came along, birds had to get themselves shot so bird-watchers could figure out what they were. With the introduction of field marks, birds could be identified where they stood, or flew—in the field, so to speak—and were left alive to go on about their business after the ordeal.

But field marks haven't been perfected. They can be annoyingly subtle. Among the *Empidonax* flycatchers, it is just about impossible to think of a single field mark that sets them apart from one another, and if you feel the urge to shoot every last one of the little bastards after you've been looking at a few of them for a while, don't feel bad. You are responding to one of the oldest of all bird-watching impulses. The field mark that distinguishes Blackpoll Warblers from Bay-breasted Warblers in the fall is the color of their legs. A Blackpoll's are a shade lighter. Now, seriously, do you have any idea how big a warbler's leg is? And the legs you are looking at are twenty-five yards away, and the light is bad. That's a terrific field mark, isn't it?

Some of them will seem ridiculously obvious. On the Blue Jay, Peterson aims his little arrows at the blue crest, the white splashes along the outer tail feathers, and the black necklace. On the other hand, if you are staring earnestly into the shadowy heart of a tree's crown and all you can see is a part of a blue, jayish bird and the part doesn't correspond to one of these three marks, it is time to start hunting around among bluish jays for likely alternatives. Unless you know what the field marks are, you're not going to know what's missing when you don't see them. Do you follow that? (A surefire way to spot an owl in a tree is to take away everything that doesn't look like an owl.)

Ideas about exactly what constitutes a field mark can be distressing. Books will go on and on in exquisite detail listing what it is about a bird that guarantees it is a Baird's Sandpiper. The reason they go on and on is because it is nearly impossible to put into words what it is about a Baird's Sandpiper that makes it different from, for example, a Western Sandpiper. Obviously, there *are* differences, and the illustrations and descriptions in the field guides may appear quite specific, but when you see scattered, whitish fluffs way the hell out on a sandbar in the middle of a sopping gale, you are going to be lucky if you can satisfy yourself that it isn't just a bunch of Kleenexes getting buffeted around.

For a while—and maybe it still is in some quarters—the term "jizz"* was extremely heavy duty. Jizz is an indefinable quality that sort of means "general impression," as long as that implies it was filtered through the sort of mystical wisdom that a Jedi Knight would bring to bear on the subject. You might hear a birder say, "It had a Henslow's jizz," or "It kind of jizzed like a Wood Thrush," although no one but a complete dork or an expert would ever let the word seriously pass their lips.

Me, I try to get what I think of as a hit, a term borrowed from the confraternity of recreational drug users. "I got a hit of Henslow" sounds a good deal less ponderous and Masonic.

A huge assortment of things can contribute to a hit. Not just the flash of a field mark or two. As unlikely as it might seem if you are just taking up the Great Game, the silhouette shape of a plover is strikingly different from the silhouette shape of any sandpiper you can name.† Flycatchers, singularly and as a group, have a shape that is unique and quite distinct from the shape of thrushes. One of the striking qualities of a bird's shape is its posture: flycatchers sit upright. Thrushes are pretty casual, by comparison. Starlings and meadowlarks *slouch*.

If the light is lousy or the weather is terrible or there are so many leaves on the trees you are going bughouse (British birders are so warped because they spend their whole lives trying to identify brown birds in

---

* Really.

† If a recreational-drug-using birder says, "I just saw a sandpiper that looked totally ploverish. Its name was Arnold," pay no attention.

heavy foliage), you will need something besides traditional field marks. Where a bird is, exactly: high in a tree, low, on the ground, in one of those rotisserie things at the supermarket. The way it perches, or stands, or whatever. If it submerges, does it sink like a submarine or fling itself forward, beak first? Its flight pattern: roller-coastery, lazy, hurried, floppy. Terns almost never glide; gulls can go miles without flapping. (The endpapers of Peterson's bird guides provide silhouettes of perched and flying birds. But don't believe everything you see in books, because from these drawings, you would never think a sensible person could confuse a kestrel and a Mourning Dove. Hah!) Does it walk or does it hop? How does it feed? These can identify a bird as precisely as feather patterns or mating song.

So, while you will be dying to crack open the field guide as soon as you see an unfamiliar bird, take it at least slightly easy and have a good look at the *real* bird. You might find yourself starting to think along the lines of ''I got a big hit of green. But it wasn't warblery. It was acting more finchy.'' You might be on your way to slam-dunking a female Painted Bunting, a call as tough as filling an inside straight.* You might be on your way to becoming a hotshot.

Going, Going . . . ? Endangered Species

When you think about how toxic we are, you and I, in all our works, it is astonishing that some birds aren't endangered.

That said, nothing is ever straightforward, including lists of endangered and threatened birds. Because of various pieces of high-caliber legislation, designation as endangered, or threatened, can cause no end of commotion around and about: for example, the Spotted Owl being threatened has caused relations between environmentalists and loggers to

---

* ''I sit here growing old by inches,
  Watching the clocks instead of the finches,
  But sometimes I visualize in my gin
  The Audubon I audubin.''
  —Ogden Nash

get a little World War Threeish amid the old-growth forests of the north-western United States. Because of the owl, these forests cannot be reduced to board feet and shipped out of there.

Artificially developed colonies of Whooping Cranes have been established in the northern and eastern states, and the population of full-blown, natural Whoopers, the ones that ply between Wood Buffalo National Park in the Northwest Territories and the Gulf Coast of Texas, is pretty well stabilized. So the bird isn't really endangered anymore. Except, the new, artificially reared Whoopers don't behave much like Whoopers, and one good hurricane or oil spill could wipe out the old, original Texas wintering grounds. Then where are we?

The Brown Pelican is on most endangered lists, but tell this to anybody who has been to Florida in the last while and they will say, "Pelicans? You can't inhale down there without getting a mouthful of pelican feathers."

The Bald Eagle is probably on the endangered list just to make people, especially Americans, feel guilty for ever having let it get the next thing to wiped out in the first place. It has actually recovered fairly handsomely.

The California Condor no longer exists, as naturalists say, in the wild, but plans are afoot to reintroduce it from the zoos where it is holding on.

And nobody has seen hide or hair of the Ivory-billed Woodpecker, Bachman's Warbler, or Eskimo Curlew for so long that if they aren't extinct, they sure as hell are good at not being watched by birders.

The endangered list is littered with subspecies: three different kinds of Clapper Rail (California, Light-footed, Yuma—all West Coast birds), but the Clapper Rail itself is more or less thriving, at least along the Gulf and Atlantic coasts. The Sandhill Crane is doing so well it is being hunted in Kansas, but the Mississippi Sandhill Crane is doing so poorly it is protected.

Canadians have additional reasons to feel sorry for themselves.* Ten full species appear on their endangered list that don't rate much more than mild anxiety in the United States. Okay, nobody's very calm about the Spotted Owl or the Piping Plover anywhere, although maybe for different reasons, but these are endangered in Canada because they are disappearing from the northern part of their range.

If the Peregrine Falcon is bouncing back from DDT, so—and who'd have thunk it? Who knew there was a problem?—is the American Robin. The falcons caught the public attention, but the danger has spread (it hasn't gone away, by any means) into species so numerous that only a few experts recognized it.

It is hard to escape the feeling that more birds get demoted to the endangered and threatened lists than get promoted—that is, get taken off the lists with clean bills of health. One thing about birding: it has its moments, but anybody who doesn't sometimes feel depressed as hell about what they see is not seeing very clearly. Aristotle might have known dick about how birds migrate, but he was loaded with attitude: "Those who are not angry at things they should be angry at are deemed fools."

When a species has been listed as endangered, it means it could become extinct in a flash. Endangered on the whole continent—and including only full species, not subspecies—are:

California Condor
Whooping Crane

* Nothing buoys us up like finding more reasons to feel sorry for ourselves.

Eskimo Curlew
Bald Eagle
Peregrine Falcon
Thick-billed Parrot
Brown Pelican
Piping Plover
Wood Stork
Least Tern
Roseate Tern
Black-capped Vireo
Bachman's Warbler
Golden-cheeked Warbler
Kirtland's Warbler
Ivory-billed Woodpecker

Species endangered, above and beyond, in Canada:

Northern Bobwhite
Harlequin Duck (eastern population)
Acadian Flycatcher
Spotted Owl
Mountain Plover
Piping Plover
King Rail
Loggerhead Shrike
Henslow's Sparrow
Sage Thrasher

For the full catastrophe, as Zorba might have called it, you can obtain *Endangered and Threatened Wildlife and Plants*—the "endangered species list," in other words—from:

U.S. Fish and Wildlife Service
Department of the Interior
1849 C Street, NW
Washington, DC 20240

In Canada, the list is called *Canadian Species at Risk*. You get it from:

> The Committee on the Status of Endangered Wildlife in Canada
> Secretariat
> Canadian Wildlife Service
> Ottawa, Ontario K1A 0H3

Gone: Extinct Species

On Tuesday, June 16, 1987, a Dusky Seaside Sparrow, a darkly hand-some subspecies of the Seaside Sparrow, which wore an orange marker band and so was known as Orange Band, died in captivity at Walt Disney World's Magic Kingdom in Orlando, Florida. The cause of death was given as old age—the bird was somewhere between ten and fifteen years old—but it might well have been love starvation. It was the last of its kind.

Actually, as a subspecies, and not a very substantial one at that (the main difference was a higher degree of melanin that accounted for its duskier hue), it could have mated with any other Seaside Sparrow or Seaside Sparrow subspecies it wanted to and carried on, more or less, but that wouldn't have been nearly so dramatic and we would have lost the maximum kitsch of where it became extinct.

Where is the poignancy in a sentence that reads, "It was the last of its vague kind"?

John K. Terres, author of the Audubon Society's majestic *Encyclopedia of North American Birds*, has a splendid eye for telling detail, and notes that since 1680, the last year of the Dodo, seventy-eight bird species have become extinct* in the world. He also has a splendid sense of indignation, as when he writes that "this continent has compiled the worst record of any comparable land mass in the world for exterminating its bird life. By

---

* One expert estimates that 1.5 million species of birds have existed since *Archaeopteryx* got into the business. A great many of these disappeared during the Miocene (meaning "well before my time") Period. Other experts find this estimate a shade high, or wildly high, or "off the clock."

contrast, Europe, with a much longer period of occupation, has not lost a single species of bird within historic times.''

The Big Nine disappearances in North America are:

The Great Auk. Like the Dodo, flightless. It was what people thought of as a penguin before penguins were discovered. Two feet high and tame as could be, Great Auks were herded aboard ships and kept like chickens to feed the crew. Their babies were good fish bait. Commercial hunters coveted Great Auk oil, and the feathers for mattress stuffing. No need to waste bullets. Great Auks were just as happy to get clubbed to death. North America's last was killed by fishermen on the Funk Islands off Newfoundland in 1841. The last in the world were killed off Iceland three years later.

The Labrador Duck. No one is really sure why it disappeared. A white sea duck of the Atlantic Coast with a black stripe up the middle of its back, it was known as the Skunk Duck and had a flavor to equal its nickname. Some were hunted for the market, and some for the hell of it, but nobody paid it much attention of any kind. The last were seen in 1875. Maybe they just lost heart.

The Passenger Pigeon. Our most famous extinction. The last, Martha Washington, went toes-up September 1, 1914, in the Cincinnati Zoo, which is where she had been born twenty-nine years before. Her ancestors had been commercially slaughtered by the kazillions for the stewpot, and if it is hard to imagine tons of butchered pigeons, it is even harder to conceive of flocks that were famous for darkening the sky and causing mighty limbs to snap off trees when they roosted. Shaped sort of like a Mourning Dove, the Passenger Pigeon was bigger, brighter-colored, and had a darkish-blue head. Apart from enormous hunting pressure,* the bird also found much of the forest where it roosted and fed cut down and cleared.

The Carolina Parakeet. For the Cincinnati Zoo, 1914 was a bad year. Not only did it lose the last Passenger Pigeon, eight months earlier the last Carolina Parakeet kicked the bucket in one of its cages. The only

---

* If the idea of shooting a pigeon for sport strikes you as odd (as opposed to shooting one because it really bugs you), remember that much of the American South finds nothing more delightful than blasting the bejeezus out of flocks of fierce Mourning Doves.

truly native North American parrot, the Carolina was big (about a foot long) and so brightly colored that its ass was always in demand to decorate women's hats. Besides that, its appetite for apples made it an appealing target for orchard growers. And besides *that*, most of its habitat—it was found throughout the East, south of the Great Lakes—got cleared.

The next five are subspecies:

The Heath Hen, the East Coast version of the Greater Prairie Chicken; the San Clemente Bewick's Wren; the Santa Barbara Song Sparrow; the Texas Henslow's Sparrow, and old Orange Band at Disney World.

And there, barring late developments regarding the Ivory-billed Woodpecker, Bachman's Warbler, and the Eskimo Curlew, is where things stand.

Good Lord, What Next? Introduced Species

In 1606, a Paris lawyer named Marc Lescarbot disembarked in New France, at Port Royal in Acadia. Things were starting to jump in this part of the world. Just down the coast in Virginia, the continent's first permanent English settlers were preparing to establish Jamestown. Lescarbot brought with him a good eye and a keen sensibility: the things he saw in the year he spent over here resulted in, among other things, his classic *Histoire de la Nouvelle-France*.

He also brought something else. Something of an eternal nature.

Columba livia.

On your checklist: Rock Dove.

The goddamned pigeon.

Lescarbot brought the pigeon from Europe with dinner in mind.* Even given that the French often take intellectual guidance from their stomachs, it is hard to think of what he did as fabulously smart. It has been downhill from there.

---

* Chickens ended up here as a result of the same sort of thinking. Thankfully, they stay fairly put. Imagine what chickens could do to a statue.

The first House Sparrows were successfully released in Brooklyn, New York, in 1851 with high expectations that the sparrows would eat the bugs that were threatening the shade trees. No doubt some human immigrants were homesick and nostalgic for the sight of the little wretches, but pest-fighting was the rationalization. All told, there were more than one hundred similar House Sparrow releases in the United States and Canada. The results? The pests that the sparrows were brought in to fight are still with us, and another pest has been added: the House Sparrow. As birds that like nesting in holes, and are not very friendly toward other birds in the same niche, they quickly chased away many native species, most notably the Eastern Bluebird, which courted extinction. And a lot of the bugs the bluebird and its fellows kept under control prospered mightily.

The lesson in this wasn't learned by the lunatics who gathered in New York's Central Park in 1890 with a cage full of fluttering birdlife. These people were inflamed with an idea that may seem strange today. They planned to introduce to North America *all the birds mentioned by Shake-*

speare. The particular item for this day in the park was the European Starling.

Here is what Shakespeare had to say about the starling. *Henry IV, Part I*. Hotspur is devising a way to annoy Mortimer:

> "And in his ear I'll holloa, *'Mortimer!'*
> Nay, I'll have a *starling* shall be taught to speak
> Nothing but *'Mortimer,'* and give it him . . ."

That's it. A fairly low moment, even for Shakespeare. And for this we have the European Starling making life noisy and dirty as long as we both shall live. Antipestilential claims were made for the starling, too. That it would eat all sorts of insects that destroyed crops. It did. Then it ate the crops. It teamed up with the House Sparrow to make life doubly hellish for the hole-nesting native species. And it moved like lightning. By 1952, it was breeding in Juneau, Alaska. By 1969, it had showed up at Inuvik, Northwest Territories, a skip from the Arctic Ocean.

There have been a lot of introductions. John L. Long, in *Introduced Birds of the World*, says attempts have been made with 119 species in North America, of which 39 proved to be splendid successes.* Among these are all kinds of game birds, such as the Ring-necked Pheasant, brought in after hunters blasted the original game to near nonexistence.

There have also been accidental introductions. The Mute Swan probably escaped from the gardens of rich folks, where it served a decorative function. Wild flocks were doing well in the East by the beginning of the twentieth century.

There have been self-introductions. For diligence and determination, nothing beats the Cattle Egret. To the best of anybody's knowledge, it flew, or got blown, to South America from Africa or southern Europe and set up housekeeping in the 1880s. By 1942, there were nest records in Florida. The first breeding Cattle Egrets in Canada were discovered in 1962.

And there have been semi-introductions. The House Finch has always

---

* By my count, Shakespeare mentioned sixty-one different birds, not counting the coistrell and the castrell, which are generally taken to be a couple of stabs at spelling "kestrel" in Elizabethan.

been at home in the southwestern United States. It moved east around 1940, when it was released on Long Island, probably by bird dealers who were dumping their stock to avoid being prosecuted when it became illegal to sell native birds. (The War on Illicit Birds? Just Say No.) Some forty-five years later, House Finches were showing up at my feeder in Toronto.

The worst of the did-it-themselves semi-introductions, or whatever, resulted in the plague of Brown-headed Cowbirds. Once confined to where the buffalo roamed, they spread everywhere as forests were cleared. The lousy parasites have successfully laid their demon spawn (devil's eggs?) in the nests of more than 140 species. If left to their own devices, they would wipe out Kirtland's Warbler in a season or two. What they're doing to other species is grim.

It was probably feeders that prompted the Northern Cardinal to introduce itself so gladly to the North. The first Canadian nesting record was at Point Pelee in 1901, and pretty well ever since it has been part of the local scene. Man did have a hand in introducing it to the southwestern United States, though, in 1880.

The government also takes a hand from time to time. The Wild Turkey has been successfully reintroduced in much of its native eastern range. In Canada, efforts to reintroduce the Trumpeter Swan to the East—where it has hardly lived in historic times—have been less than roaringly successful. Trumpeter Swan eggs have been stuck under nesting Mute Swans in the hopes that the Mutes might become foster parents, but the Mute Swan is just as miserable about this as it is about everything else.

Passerine

There aren't many birding terms you need to know that are not in ordinary English, but "passerine" is one. It refers to a huge order of birds properly known as "Passeriformes." "Passerine" itself is from *passerinus*, a Latin word that meant "sparrows," more or less. It has come to mean "perching birds." This is useful, because "passerine" clearly doesn't include grebes, since grebes never perch. But it's not *that* useful, because Great Blue Herons are first-class perchers, and so are Wood Storks, and if there are two things that are definitely not passerines, they are Great Blue Herons and Wood Storks.

So now what? The suborder of passerines that are of particular interest to us are the Oscines,* or singing birds. (Skulking in the Latin background of "Oscine" is *canere*: to sing.) Often when people use the word "passerine" (people almost never speak of Oscines unless they hold a tenured position), they aren't talking about a perching bird, but about a songbird. But try telling this to the proud nonpasserine parents of a Whip-poor-will that think it is the next Willie Nelson.

It comes down to this: The fact that a bird perches or sings doesn't make it one of the perching songbirds known as "passerines."

Where is the line drawn, then? In the field guides, it is drawn right smack between woodpeckers and flycatchers.

Passerines—everything from flycatchers on, going by the book—are regarded as the last word in bird design. The most evolved. The most evolving, since this is where most of the action in current bird evolution is taking place. And they are certainly regarded as the brainiest: the biggest passerine of all, the Common Raven, is generally thought to be the Thomas Edison of feathered friends. All passerines have the same kind of feet: four toes, three forward, and a particularly strong one backward that makes gripping a branch a cinch. A number of commentators mention that passerines have distinctive sperm, although what is so distinctive about it is unclear to the lay reader, i.e., me.

Passerines run up and down the scales of behavior. While most of them get by on seeds and bugs and worms, they include birds that are quite happy to raid nests for their eggs (grackles, for one), and to kill smaller birds for their internal organs (grackles, for two). Shrikes are admirably bloodthirsty for songbirds, birds of prey in all but scientific classification. The American Dipper spends much of its life not only in the water, but under it. And the House Sparrow went into severe decline† when the horse disappeared from city streets, taking its road apples with it.

---

* Birders have hours of good fun debating the merits of nine-primaried Oscines.

† Hard to imagine that the current House Sparrow situation is an example of severe decline, but there you are.

The other birding term that is not in ordinary English but is something you need to know is "goatsucker," but I hardly feel that this is the place to discuss it. Perhaps if I knew you better.

Species

According to the authorities, a birder who worked at it could find 838 species of birds in North America. Of these, 116 are considered accidental or casual visitors. There are thought to be roughly nine thousand species in the world today, although some experts estimate as high as ten thousand.*

Bird books are obliged to explain that when it comes to species, we are at the mercy of a bunch of busybodies known as "lumpers" and "splitters." For some time, the lumpers seemed to be running the asylum. That is why the Myrtle Warbler and the Audubon's Warbler no longer exist, having been lumped into the Yellow-rumped Warbler. Now they are into a splitting fit: the Western Grebe has become the Western Grebe and Clark's Grebe.† If the Baltimore Oriole is neurotic, it's because it has been lumped and unlumped, one right after the other. The official busybodies had lumped it with Bullock's Oriole into a dreary smudge called the Northern Oriole. This despite the fact that the Baltimore and Bullock's look only vaguely like one another and weren't especially fond of one another in the middle of the continent, where they overlapped. After barely twenty years of lumpedness, the busybodies split them up again.‡

Human beings are a species of mammal. We humans are divided into a

---

* Jonathan Weiner, in *The Beak of the Finch*, says there are 9,672 species of birds in the world today. Nothing wishy-washy about that number. It has "no dicking around" written all over it. It is a capital-N Number. Absolutely.

† A lump hurts because it means losing a bird from your life list. The idea that lumpers are beating out splitters could be birders' paranoia. There is no shortage of that.

‡ The busybodies like to suggest that Baltimore and Bullock's have gone their separate ways in "a nice example of evolution over a short period." They don't like to suggest that the birds were going their separate ways all along and were lumped in the first place simply to irritate birders.

bunch of different groups called "races," but these are no big deal. Any member of any race can breed with any member of any other race* and produce kiddies that are the apples of their parents' eyes, providing they keep their noses clean. Except for one or two minor characteristics—biologically, skin color is small potatoes—all our races are pretty much the same.

All birds have similarities, as do all mammals, so we shouldn't be surprised that an Ostrich and a hummingbird are both birds. But when you look at certain groups of birds—for instance, all those yellowish kingbirds in the West—you have to say they look so much alike it is hard to believe they aren't just different races (or subspecies; it is the same thing. To become an official subspecies, a bird needs to have developed a certain percentage of different characteristics) of the same species. To the barenaked eye, they look far more like each other than the different races of humans do; than most brothers and/or sisters do, as a matter of fact. But they are considered entirely separate species. A Western Kingbird and a Cassin's Kingbird might as well be an elk and a gerbil when it comes to intimacy.

They probably started out as one species, though, and ended up all over the genetic map because of the way species are formed. Allow me to simplify. (If you don't believe in evolution, ignore everything from here on.) Let's imagine the first full, official, actual, not-even-slightly reptilian bird. It was probably quite a bit like a loon, and can be considered the first bird *species*. What we have to work out is how to get from this one loony species to nine thousand or so species—not races, but separate species—as different as Turkey Vultures and Northern Cardinals.

It went something like this: As the old neighborhood gets crowded, some loons move south. Over time, the heat of the sun and the temperature of the water make these southerners look different. Different kinds of fish are on their menu. Over time, the southerners develop different ways of coming on to each other. They enjoy different music. They can interbreed with northerners, but as time goes on, they find they are more attracted to the loons that have the same courtship rituals as they do, and sing the songs they know best.

---

* Taking gender into account. Don't go reading anything radical into this.

If they keep going their separate ways, they'll forget all about inter-breeding, and even if they give it a whirl, it won't come to much.

Bingo! Two species.

Loons are lousy walkers, but one year when fish is in short supply, a couple of loons that have sturdier legs discover there is good grub onshore. These landlubber loons start hanging around with one another, and soon produce generations of children that are nearly as at home on land. Like geese.

Three species.

Along comes continental drift. North America and Europe break apart, right down the middle of a flock of geese. Half go east, half go west, half fly over the cuckoo's nest. Wait, wrong story. There aren't any cuckoos yet. Anyway, they end up becoming separate species. Some of these geese wander into the desert, and those among their offspring that behave like Ostriches do much better. They forget how to fly. They become Ostriches.

A mountain chain springs up in the middle of another flock of geese. The ones stranded on the other side discover that pecking insects out of the bark of trees is the only way to survive. Along comes an ice age. Glaciers drive a big wedge through this flock of woodpeckers. The ones on one side keep on pecking wood. The ones on the other side say the hell with this, and start pouncing on geese and loons and eating them raw. The woodpeckers that develop hooked bills and huge talons are better at this than the ones that don't. They become eagles.

It doesn't always have to be something cataclysmic. Maybe a big wind blows a flock of these eagles off to where there is nothing to eat but flies. It is awkward for an eagle to catch a fly. The smaller eagles do better, especially the ones as small as pewees. And so on.

It might be that the oriole ancestors of the Bullock's and Baltimore, all of them looking exactly alike, got separated during an ice age. This headed them in the direction of becoming distinct species. One of the first things to change when groups of birds separate is their looks; minor color variations that would normally get bred out of the broader popula-tion might get bred in and become fashionable in the separated popula-tion. But they lost their separate status when at least some of them were discovered overlapping in more ways than one. The Audubon's and Myrtle Warblers might have been split apart when the Rocky Mountains thrust up from wherever they thrust up from. They got lumped after it was discovered that when they got together, they couldn't keep their buttons buttoned.

Assignment to a species can cause arguments. In *American Warblers*, Douglass H. Morse writes that when it came to our warblers, "as recently as 1885, the great British ornithologist R. Bowdler Sharpe, in his *Catalogue of Birds of the British Museum*, accepted the family, but reluctantly, and predicted that it would be found an unnatural one. He suggested that *Vermivora* and the 'brown warblers' were wrens, the Yellow-breasted Chat was a vireo, the American Redstart and other flycatching warblers were Old World flycatchers, and tropical forms were tanagers."

In the beginning, Darwin was vague and conflicted. He started off believing species was a thoroughly arbitrary notion invented to make life easier for scientists who can't stand things that aren't classified. Then he swung around to the assumption that species were so separate that if they made it with each other, their offspring—the hybrids—would be sterile, like mules.

Our most famous hybrid birds are the offspring of the Blue-winged and the Golden-winged Warblers known as Brewster's Warbler and Lawrence's Warbler. There is a belief among many birders that Brewster's and Lawrence's are mules, incapable of reproduction, but like a number of birding beliefs, this one isn't worth much. There was a time when Lawrence's and Brewster's were thought to be actual species themselves; now it turns out there are all kinds of other hybrids that fall in between the way the parents look and the way these do, but you can't see these differences without your Ph.D. That aside, since they are as fertile as need be, why don't we see pure lines of Brewster's and of Lawrence's showing up?

We don't because they have a hard time getting dates. First off, they are naturally inclined to get the hots for Blue-wingeds and Golden-wingeds (call it imprinting, call it . . . *tradition*), which, as objects of affection, might not appreciate getting their bones jumped by something that looks like a complete stranger. Second, there are so few of them, and they are so widely scattered, that it is tough for, say, a Brewster's to find a like-minded Brewster's of the appropriate sex so they can go about producing a tribe of purer Brewster's Warblers. If they manage to mate at all, it is almost certainly with one of the parent species, and the hybrid characteristics blur out of existence in a generation or two.

For a long time, this Blue-winged/Golden-winged thing was thought to be a unique thing, but now it looks as if all kinds of different species* go after anything they can get, but nothing comes of it, or what does fizzles out in a year or two. Anyway, they don't get the chance all that often. Almost everything about a species, from color to feather pattern to song to courtship ritual, appeals pretty specifically to members of the same species. Whole new species don't pop up very often.

Just to make everything perfectly bewildering, there is a rising school of thought that is phylogenetic as opposed to biological. As far as I can figure out, this nasty mouthful means that a species is made of direct descendants, sort of the way the royal family is. By this measure, Red-shafted and Yellow-shafted Flickers would be separate species, and not simply subspecies. Their ability to interbreed like bunnies is only one trait and not the whole ball game.

But while species can be an awful lot like each other and might be able to interbreed successfully whenever they want to, something in the long run keeps them from being very interested in doing it. Why this should be (why all Darwin's finches haven't just melted back into one finch) is another entry on the checklist of abiding mysteries.

Zen and the Curlew Sandpiper

"In the beginner's mind there are many possibilities; in the expert's mind there are few."—*Shunryu Suzuki*

It was only a few months after I began birding that I went to bird-watching heaven, Point Pelee in early May. Toward the end of each day there, the diehards move north of the park, beyond the legendary onion fields, to a splatter of marshes where they scan the distant reedbeds and

---

* Paul R. Ehrlich is driven to italics when he defines species as "organisms that are distinctly different from others *and do not ordinarily interbreed* with individuals of other species."

sandbars. There, in a phalanx, shoulder to shoulder with the grizzled veterans, I stood, my scope one of a dozen trained across the brown water. My eye drifted along the the milling hundreds of dowitchers and Dunlin and . . . *What in the name of . . . ?!* I came upon a bird that looked, it seemed to me, the tiniest bit peculiar. In the fading light, I peered hard as I could at it, then drew forth my trusty Peterson and squinted at all the mystifying possibilities. And kept returning to one. Could it be? I looked back through the scope, went back to the book. Back to the scope, back to the book. Scope. Book. Scope. Book. Until finally there was no doubt at all.

"Curlew Sandpiper," I announced quite proudly because it was the first time in such exalted, and competitive, company I had been the first to call a bird, any bird at all.

"*Shhhh!*" hissed my guru. I thought he was going to clamp his hand over my mouth. He was astonishingly agitated. He glanced around at the other birders. "*Shhhhh!*"

"Whatsamatter?" I whispered.

"Be careful or somebody will hear you!" he whispered back.

"Whaddya talking about? I got a Curlew Sandp—"

"*SHHHHHH!* For God's sake!"

"I ha—"

"Don't joke about something like that! Not here!"

"I'm not jo—"

"Will you *shut up!*"

"Look for yourself."

"Where?"

"There!" I checked again. "In the middle of my scope."

He scrunched over and looked through my scope. He looked for a long time. Night grew nigher. At last he straightened up and turned to me. "Listen," he said. "You'll look like a complete idiot if you call a bird like that in front of all these people and it's the wrong call."

"Well, what's that goddamn bird?" Imagine a voice pitched between novice indignation and the desire not to be mortified for the rest of your life.

"All I could see were dowitchers and Dunlin," he said.

I looked back through the scope. The shapes had become nothing but dark blobs. Blobs blobbing together, becoming blobbier. The wind was making my eyes water. I could barely see anything at all. Over the wind came the clattery racket of tripod legs being telescoped and folded. Behind me, footsteps crunched off the beach. I was slow to leave.

It was the last day of my visit to Pelee. Late that night, unable to sleep, I pulled Peterson out again and looked at the picture. It sure looked right. By the light of my guttering candle, I read the text, something I had neglected to do before. "Note the slim, *downcurved bill*" . . . yup . . . *"whitish rump"* . . . yup, yup . . . "bill *curved slightly down throughout."* Yup, yup, yup. "Main distinction is the *whitish rump.*" Yup, yup, yup, yup, yup. Damn it. Yup.

Then I read, "Range: E. Arctic Asia. Migrant to Africa. East: Rare straggler to e. N. America."

What?! What was that? I read it again. The words blazed in my brain until you could smell the smoke. I dug out the official, government-issued Point Pelee checklist. *There was no Curlew Sandpiper on it!*

In front of the assembled priests of bird-dom I had tried to call a bird that probably had never existed in that neck of the woods.

What a fool I had been. What an idiot.

There was only one thing to do.

I stuck my binoculars in the bottom drawer of my bureau and gave up bird-watching. Weeks passed. The memory of my humiliation began to fade. Life, as best it could, limped on. I started buying the *Racing Form.*

Some months later, I encountered my guru again and he told me what he believed to be the most amazing story. "I got to tell you the most amazing story" is how he put it. He said the day after I left Point Pelee, a couple of real hotshots at the marsh had found a Curlew Sandpiper away out on the sandbars. Imagine! A Curlew Sandpiper! *The day after I left!* It got rave reviews. It drew enormous crowds. My guru felt kind of sorry for me, sorry I hadn't been there on the right day, sorry that I had been *in the exact spot* where a splendid birding experience was about to happen *the very next day*, but I had been there on the *wrong* day. Of all the rotten luck. Oh, well, isn't that how it goes in birding?

To this day I don't have a Curlew Sandpiper on my life list. When I run into my guru, I get a bit terse.

The Hit List

Down & Dirty's *surefire tricks for figuring out*
which damn bird is which 🌿 *Well, maybe at least*
you'll be able to tell the Cactus Wren
from the cactus

The basic rule of birding is: The twitchier you are, the quicker you will stop looking at a new bird and start looking it up in your field guide.

That isn't actually the rule. The real rule is: As soon as you start looking a bird up in your field guide, the real bird will fly away.

The point of the rule is: The less time you spend looking at the real bird, the less you will remember about what it looked like, and the harder it will be to find in your field guide.

In other words: If you want to make sure you will *never* figure out what a bird is, start looking it up in the book the minute you lay eyes on it.

Take it easy. Take in as much of the bird as you can while you've got the bird to take in. Even then, identification is no cinch.

What I'm listing in this section are the one or two hits you might get from a bird that will most help you figure out what the bird is. I've tried to pick the things that should stick in your mind—things you might remember more than anything else. To get any use out of this list (and to make any sense out of it), you will need a real field guide, one with pictures and full descriptions of all the different species. Throughout, I pretty well follow the order set out in the National Geographic's *Field Guide to the Birds of North America*. To some extent, I'm suggesting the places where Roger Tory Peterson's field mark arrows might go if they were sprinkled on the National Geographic's illustrations. And I've tried to come up with useful distinctions between, and among, closely related species. Sometimes, these are so subtle they make you goofy.

Some things you should know about colors: Colors can be bewildering. The texts of bird guides always sound so positive, and the pictures always look so clear. Birds, on the other hand, show up in all sorts of lousy conditions—bad light, driving rain—and in costumes that can be bedraggled, dirty, worn-out, sun-bleached, soaking wet, or just plain contrary.

In bird descriptions, nothing is more confusing than red. It can be red, ruddy, rufous, rusty, reddish, russet. Sometimes, chestnut gets thrown into the mix.

There are all kinds of green: green, greenish, lime green, olive, olivaceous, blue-green. In any but perfect light, green turns into something else. Often black.

There is light brown, there is buffy, there is cinnamon, there is brown, there is dark brown. There is also chestnut.

Gray. You would think gray was gray and brown was brown, but in birds and bird descriptions and bird illustrations, you wouldn't want to bet on it. Look up Wrentit in the National Geographic field guide. ''A perky little brown bird,'' it says. ''Plumage varies from reddish-brown in northern populations to grayish in southern birds.'' From the pictures, it looks grayish in all birds. I don't see any ''brown.'' A little ruddy, or rufous in the breast of the northern birds, I can see. But this the book calls ''buffy.'' Maybe I'm color-blind. Maybe I'm crazy.

Some things you should know about size: For easy reference, the standard bird sizes are sparrow-sized, robin-sized, crow-sized, and chicken-sized. Sparrows come in a whole bunch of sizes, but don't go getting tight-assed. Think of sparrows in general. That is sparrow-sized. Anyway, the sooner you figure out what these different sizes are, the easier things will be. It isn't very hard.

What's hard is remembering that YOU ABSOLUTELY CANNOT— you see that? Capital letters! YOU ABSOLUTELY CANNOT—tell how big an unfamiliar bird is when it is off by itself. You think you can, but you can't. You will come up with egg on your kisser every time you fail to remember this.

The size rule: Without something to judge size against, you can't judge size.

Corollary to the size rule: You will fail to remember the rule.

Degree, which is sort of like size, is relevant to many things. Down

among the thrashers in this list, you will see that I say the only notable
difference between the Curve-billed Thrasher and Bendire's Thrasher is
that the Curve-billed's bill is curvier. Since you are not likely to see the
two of them together very often, this useful-sounding bit of direction
turns out to be *almost no use at all*.

Another thing: Don't be shy about scribbling all sorts of notes,
reminders, hints, and whatevers in your field guide. It might take you
ages to look up the key difference between soaring Cooper's and Sharp-
shinned Hawks, but if you've written it beside their pictures, you'll
remember right away. Field guides are useful, but if you want to make
them really useful, you have to start modifying them with your own hard-
won wisdom.

Every bird in the National Geographic guide is not on this list. There
is no mistaking some birds: a male Blackburnian Warbler, a Prothonotary Warbler. You can figure those out on your own. A Roseate
Spoonbill doesn't look like anything else. And some birds don't hang
around places that the average new birder hangs around, and by the
time you encounter them, you will be such a hotshot you won't need
this book. But all kinds of fairly common birds look so much alike it is
almost hopeless: all the crows, for instance. This is where you might
pick up some quick tricks. Anyway, if a bird is not listed, it's because
you're not all that likely to run across it, or it is so obvious it would be
a waste of time, or I forgot.

The Hit List

Loons

Common Loon vs. Yellow-billed Loon vs. Pacific Loon vs. Red-throated
Loon. Pacific and Red-throated have pale heads in breeding plumage. Red-
throated and Yellow-billed have bills that point somewhat *up*.

Grebes

Western Grebe vs. Clark's Grebe. Western is masked like Zorro.
Clark's isn't.

Horned Grebe vs. Eared Grebe. In winter, the Eared has a dark ear patch.

Albatrosses, Shearwaters, Etc.

By the time you are out cruising the oceans on a pelagic bird-watching jaunt or tootling around their nesting territories, you will probably know what you are looking for. Is this a cop-out or what?

Wilson's Storm-Petrel.* Is likely the storm-petrel following your cruise liner. Walks on the water.

Frigatebirds

Magnificent Frigatebird. Sailing overhead it is all sharp angles and menace. If you see the red throat inflated, you are lucky.

Pelicans

American White Pelican vs. Brown Pelican. The White Pelican hunts in fleets. The Brown dives headfirst into the water.

A thought: Big white soaring birds with black trim on wings.
    White Pelican. Black tips and trailing edge.
    Wood Stork. Black tips and trailing edge.
    Whooping Crane. Only primaries are black; that is, the trailing edge is black only halfway down wing from tip.

Gannets and Boobies

Northern Gannet. Has a goldish wash to the back of its head.
Brown Booby. Likely the booby following your ship. Yellow bill, yellow feet.

Anhingas

Anhinga. It soars with the hawks, it swims, it dives, it floats with only its neck out of the water so it looks like a snake, it clambers around in trees, it opens its wings and hangs them out to dry like a cormorant. Talk about a repertoire.

---

* Once thought to be the most abundant bird species of all, it has been overtaken by the Red-billed Quelea, which has an estimated breeding population in Africa—and only in Africa, thank goodness—of 1.5 billion.

Cormorants

Cormorants all look like cormorants. Cormorants flying look like they have had both ends in a pencil sharpener.

Double-crested Cormorant. The one you see in the interior of the continent. I have never been able to see its two crests.

Great Cormorant. Has a white chin.

Olivaceous Cormorant. There is a little white stripe at the back of its jaw. But forget that. Just look for a tiny cormorant.

Pelagic Cormorant. Tiny, too. Skinny straight neck. Has white patches on its flank.

Brandt's Cormorant. A blue throat pouch it is proud of in breeding. Heavy-headed, cormorant that doesn't fit any other category.

Red-faced Cormorant. Pale bill.

Herons

Herons fly with their necks folded back. Storks and cranes don't. Lots of herons have shortish necks, so it's not something that always strikes you right off. With the big ones, though, it counts for something.

Least Bittern. Teeny. Size of a spindly robin.

American Bittern. Pointy wings, for a heron. Brown back.

Black-crowned Night-Heron vs. Yellow-crowned Night-Heron. In flight, the Black-crowned's feet, and only its feet, extend beyond its tail, while the Yellow-crowned's feet *and* a length of leg bone stick out. This way, you can tell which is which no matter what plumage they are in. It may be true.

Green-backed Heron. Don't expect green that is all that greeny.

Tricolored Heron. White stripe down front of its throat.

Little Blue Heron. Immatures are white. Immatures have pale blue bills with black tips.

Reddish Egret. Even if it happens to be white, which it occasionally is, the adult will have a pink bill with a black tip.

Cattle Egret. Stubby bill.

Snowy Egret. Black legs, yellow feet. Black bill.

Great Egret. Black legs, black feet.

Great Blue Heron. If happens to be white, which it, too, occasionally is, its legs are pale. Otherwise, it always looks like a Great Blue Heron.

Storks

Wood Stork. White plumage with black trailing edges and a head the size of a sledgehammer. Flies with neck stretched out.

Ibises

Glossy Ibis vs. White-faced Ibis. Nicely separated on the map. The White-faced is reddish of bill, and reddish around the eye.

Cranes

Sandhill Crane vs. Whooping Crane. No contest. The Sandhill is gray. Cranes fly with their necks stretched out.

Swans

Tundra Swan vs. Trumpeter Swan vs. Mute Swan. The Tundra's neck goes pretty well straight up from its shoulders. (Do birds have shoulders?) The Trumpeter's neck is a bit hunched back on its shoulders. The Mute has the S-curvy neck and is very Shakespearean, but watch it. It might be pretty as a picture, but a Mute Swan will attack your dog. It will break your wrist.

Geese

If it is grazing on land, the same as a cow or a horse, it is a goose.

Greater White-fronted Goose. A mostly gray goose.

Snow Goose. A big white goose with black wing tips, unless it is one of the Blue Goose types, and then it still keeps a white head.

Ross's Goose. A little white goose—with a much daintier bill—unless it is of the bluish persuasion, and then it has a black Mohawk cut.

Emperor Goose. Black chin, white head.

Canada Goose. A goose of many shapes and sizes. On the Bering Coast of Alaska, it is hardly bigger than a duck. In all cases, it has the black head, the black neck, the white chin.

Brant Goose. A faint white filigree under its jaw; otherwise, it's black from the breast up. Canada Goose's black starts at the neck.

Ducks (Dabblers)

Dabblers don't dive to feed.* Sometimes, when they feed off the bottom, they stick their heads under water and their buns straight up in the air. They don't have to taxi to take off but can leap into the air from a sitting start.

Mallard vs. American Black Duck vs. Mottled Duck. The Mallard is the basic duck. Note the kiss curls at the tips of the male's tail coverts. Cute or what? In the right sort of light, the female Mallard looks exactly like the American Black and the Mottled Duck. The Mallard has white lines on each side of its speculum. The Black's underwings flash silvery in flight.

Gadwall. The male is a symphony in monochrome. Check the all-black tush. In bad light, the female looks like a female Mallard, but has a white speculum.

American Wigeon. Now that I think of it, most female dabblers look like female Mallards. Wigeons feed prissily, as if picking lint off the water's surface.

Northern Shoveler vs. Ruddy Duck. The Shoveler is a jazzy Mallard. It and the Ruddy have bills that look as if they were drawn by cartoonists. (So does the Canvasback.) In winter, the Ruddy has a big white cheek patch.

Whistling Ducks

Black-bellied Whistling-Duck vs. Fulvous Whistling-Duck. The Black-bellied has a black belly and an orange bill. The Fulvous doesn't.

Diving Ducks (Pochards)

Canvasback vs. Redhead. Canvasback has the goofy bill. Redhead has a gray hull.

Ring-necked Duck. The neck ring is invisible to the human eye. The ring you see is near the tip of its bill.

Greater Scaup vs. Lesser Scaup. Some books swear by a greenish tinge to the head for the Greater, and a purplish for the Lesser. Some books swear by head shapes—rounder for Greater, pointier for Lesser. I swear I can't tell them apart.

* They know how to dive. It's just that they prefer not to.

Diving Ducks (Eiders)

Common Eider vs. King Eider. The King Eider female's flanks are less stripy and more like pointy scales than the Common female's.

Diving Ducks (Sea Ducks)

Oldsquaw. I only mention them here to point out their skill at landing. They are crash-landers.* If you are a klutz, they will make you feel good all over.

Diving Ducks (Mergansers)

Common Merganser vs. Red-breasted Merganser. The Common male has the round head. The Common female has a sharp line separating its red throat from its white breast. The Red-breasted female's breast is blah all the way up. Don't expect much of a *red* breast on anybody.

Hooded Mergansers. Have dark bills.

Rails

King Rail vs. Virginia Rail vs. Clapper Rail. By standard measure, the King is two handfuls, the Virginia one handful. If you see a very dull King and you are not inland, you might have a Clapper.

Sora vs. Yellow Rail. If you say, "That looks like some kind of chicken," it is a Sora. A Sora with a dark bill and a pale throat could be a Yellow.

Gallinules and Coots

Purple Gallinule vs. Common Moorhen vs. American Coot. The gallinule has a pale-blue thingy between its eyes. Besides, it's purple, for God's sake. The moorhen is blackish with a red thingy between its eyes. The coot has a white bill.

Jacanas

Northern Jacana. If it is walking *on* the lily pads, it's probably a Jacana.

Stilts and Avocets

American Avocet vs. Black-necked Stilt. Avocet's bill curves up. Stilt's bill is straight. Avocets hunt in gangs, like White Pelicans.

---

* You would think they would have got it right by now.

Plovers

Before anything else, ask yourself these simple questions.

1. How many neckbands?
2. Does the neckband go all the way around?
3. What if it looks like a plover but has no neckband?

(Note: Exempted from this test are the Black-bellied Plover and the Lesser Golden-Plover. They are a different kettle of whatnot.)

Killdeer. If it has two neckbands, it is only a lousy Killdeer.

Wilson's Plover, Semipalmated Plover, and Common Ringed Plover. Have only one band. Wilson's has a big black bill. As between the Semipalmated and the Common, the Common is said to have a broader band at the front.

Piping Plover. The band is usually only complete on a breeding male, but not always. The rest of the bird is pale, pale, pale.

Snowy Plover. Neckband never goes all the way around.

Mountain Plover. No neckband.

Black-bellied Plover vs. Lesser Golden-Plover. The Black-bellied has black armpits. In breeding plumage, its black belly is white from the waist down. The Lesser Golden-Plover wouldn't be caught dead with black armpits and, just to confuse you, in breeding has a black belly that goes right to the bottom.

Sandpipers

Most sandpipers are migrating through when we see them, so pictures of them in high breeding plumage are mainly of academic interest. Most of us see them when they are dull, dull, dull. They come in three general categories: Great Big Sandpipers, Middle-sized Sandpipers, and "Peeps." They are known as "peeps" because after you have looked at a mudflat with a thousand of them on it for an hour and haven't been able to figure out what they are, you are reduced to thinking of them in a pitiful, whimpering way that is best expressed—on the off chance that there is polite company in the vicinity—in a strangled shriek: "You peeps!"

Great Big Sandpipers

Marbled Godwit vs. Bar-tailed Godwit vs. Hudsonian Godwit. Godwit bills curve *up*.* Marbled has cinnamon wing lining. The Bar-tailed's tail is definitely striped. Or barred. The Hudsonian has a black tail and a white rump.

Bristle-thighed Curlew. You must be standing on the Bering coast of Alaska.

Whimbrel. A great big sandpiper with a bill that curves down and a notably stripy head.

Long-billed Curlew. Happy standing around in parks. It is the biggest great big sandpiper of all, as big as a chicken. It doesn't need field marks.

Middle-Sized Sandpipers

Willet. Dull till it flashes its chic black-and-white underwings.

Greater Yellowlegs vs. Lesser Yellowlegs. They have yellow legs. My feeling is you can't tell Greater from Lesser by sight, and it's no cinch by sound. But suit yourself.

Solitary Sandpiper. Look for a white eye-ring. Bobs its tail a bit.

Spotted Sandpiper. Bobs everything. It is the one sandpiper that is nearly everywhere in breeding season. It has no spots after breeding. Then the mark is the white shoulder patch.

Wandering Tattler. One very gray bird.

Phalaropes

The only sandpipers that regularly *swim*. Definitely the only sandpipers that spin around on the water as if they have lost their marbles. They are only hard to separate in nonbreeding gear.

Wilson's Phalarope vs. Red-necked Phalarope vs. Red Phalarope. The one that is handy to most folks in breeding season is Wilson's. In nonbreeding, it is the one with the white rump and without the really dark smudge through the eye. In winter, the Red-necked might have more of a dark cap than the Red, and a streakier back. The Red is more inclined to male-pattern baldness.

Dowitchers

When dowitchers feed, their bills move like sewing machine needles.

---

* Curlew and Whimbrel bills curve down. Wasn't this thoughtful of Nature?

Short-billed Dowitcher vs. Long-billed Dowitcher. You might be able to pick which is which by ear, but in migration, they're not given to saying much. Be generously skeptical of anybody who says they can tell dowitchers apart by sight, even with one of each standing side by side.

Stilt Sandpiper. Often feeds like a dowitcher in deeper water. A hint of down-curve at the bill's tip. A hint of white eyebrow.

Common Snipe. Zigzags like crazy when it takes off. Stripy head.

American Woodcock. Stripes on head go crosswise. Almost as round as a Frisbee when it flies.

Ruddy Turnstone. The only turnstone you see in the East. Off breeding, it keeps its paint-by-numbers outline. Turnstones *turn stones over*.

Surfbird vs. Rock Sandpiper vs. Purple Sandpiper. Wintry versions look depressingly alike. The Purple is the only one that shows up in the East. Seems short-legged. The Surfbird has a white rump and tail with a wide black band near the end, and a stubby bill.

Red Knot. Easy in breeding, with its robin-red breast. Otherwise, roundish like a dowitcher, but altogether paler—white breast. Shorter-billed.

Dunlin. A dinky little down-curve at the tip of the bill. Not a lot to go on. If you're lucky, a hint of the black belly.

Sanderling. When civilians think of sandpipers, they think of Sanderlings, the funny little fellows running back and forth, chasing the wash of waves along the beach, tra-la.

Pectoral Sandpiper. A handsome tweedy dickey pulled down to the middle of its breast.

Upland Sandpiper. Whoever called it the Pigeon-headed Sandpiper knew what they were doing. The only breeding sandpiper regularly strewn about fields in the countryside. When it lands, it holds its wings straight up for a second.

Buff-breasted Sandpiper. It would be cheap to say that if it is none of the above, it is a Buff-breasted. They are buffy. A dry-land bird in migration.

Peeps

Semipalmated. Western. Least. White-rumped. Baird's. Aiyee! It might help you to know that the only ones that winter over—they do it along the south coast—are the Western and Least. But it won't help much.

Skuas and Jaegers

Skuas you don't see without considerable effort.

Pomarine Jaegers vs. Parasitic Jaeger vs. Long-tailed Jaeger. Pomarines and Parasitics are sometimes seen way out on the Great Lakes. Pomarines have central tail plumes shaped like Popsicle sticks. Flight heavy and slow. Parasitic and Long-tailed have lighter, ternlike flight. The migrating Long-tailed is almost never seen by shorebound birders.

Gulls

There is no such thing as a seagull.* I stick with adults here, because immature gulls are a lifetime's work. There are three-year gulls, four-year gulls. Unless you're doing your doctorate, leave it to the gulls to figure out which they are.

Hooded Gulls

Are only hooded in breeding season; in between, the hood dissolves into a variety of seedy decoration.

Franklin's Gull. If it is on the Central Plains in breeding season, it is Franklin's.
Laughing Gull. A Gulf Coast, East Coast bird; dark-footed, noisy.
Bonaparte's Gull. Streamlined, elegant. *Skips* through the air.
Common Black-headed Gull. Has a *brown* hood. Adult has red legs.
Little Gull. Only the Little has a slaty underwing. Light flight.
Sabine's Gull. Very slightly forked tail. Black bill has yellow tip. Triangle-patched, three-toned wings.

Hoodless Gulls

Heermann's Gull. Very gray of breast in all plumages.
Ross's Gull. Worth the trip to Churchill, Manitoba, where it is slightly bigger than the mosquitoes. Pinker when it's horny. Wedgy tail.
Ring-billed Gull. Has a black ring about a quarter-inch from the bill tip. Yellow legs. Loves freshly plowed fields, McDonald's parking lots.
Mew Gull. Dinky little bill.

---

* For a while, the actress Barbara Hershey called herself Barbara Seagull. But then she gave it up. This kind of thing went on in the seventies.

Herring Gull. Big. Big yellow bill. Pink legs.

California Gull. A Herring Gull with yellow legs. There is a black zit beside the red dot on its bill.

Glaucous vs. Glaucous-winged. Adult Glaucous has light eye, Glaucous-winged, dark eye. That's not a lot to go on, is it? In the East, it is the Glaucous. Unless it is a rare, stray Glaucous-winged.

Iceland vs. Thayer's. Iceland has light iris. It is found East and North. Thayer's has dark iris. It is found West and North. They divide Baffin Island pretty well down the middle.*

Lesser Black-backed Gull. Don't expect a *black* back. A Herring Gull with a bolder fashion sense, yellow legs.

Great Black-backed Gull. Now *this* is a black back. It is also huge. We are talking turkey. Pinkish legs.

Western Gull. Smaller and less flashy than Great Black-backed. Bigger and flashier than Lesser Black-backed. It doesn't matter. They're eastern, this is western.

Red-legged Kittiwake vs. Black-legged Kittiwake. Red-legged has red legs. Black-legged has you guessed it. Pigeony bills. They only mix in Alaska; everywhere else, it is Black-legged.

Terns

Terns are pointier than gulls. They don't glide as much as gulls. They are flappers. They get such a boost from each flap that they seem to spring through the air. This sort of light, bounding flight is known as "ternlike." Terns don't sit around on the water the way gulls do. Terns dive headfirst into water after little fish. It would be a very weird gull that dived headfirst into the water after anything.

Common Tern vs. Forster's Tern vs. Arctic Tern. Only Forster's winters in the United States. Experts focus on the relative darkness of the primaries. When I say I see what the experts are talking about, I am not being completely honest. Forster's is marshier. Arctic's bill is all dark orange.

Aleutian Tern. White forehead.

Roseate Tern. Just don't expect to see it roseate. Bill mainly black.

* They are welcome to it.

Gull-billed Tern. Heavy black bill.
Least Tern. A teeny tern with a white forehead.
Black Tern. Black body and grayish wings.

The following terns are getting on for gull-sized. For medium-sized gull-sized, anyway.

Sandwich Tern. A long, skinny black bill with a yellow tip.
Elegant vs. Royal Tern. A challenge. No Elegants in East.
Caspian Tern. Getting more common inland. A great big red-orange honker.

Auks and Puffins

The world of Razorbills, murres, Dovekies, guillemots, murrelets, auklets, and puffins is yours to discover.*

Vultures

Vultures are not buzzards, but are what most people think of when they think of buzzards. They are what western movies call buzzards. "Buzzard" is actually a corruption of *Buteo*. The European equivalent of the Rough-legged Hawk is called the Rough-legged Buzzard. Vultures are vultures.

Turkey Vulture vs. Black Vulture. TV glides with its wings in a broad V. This is called a "dihedral." It is a tippy glider, wobbling from side to side. The undersides of its primaries and secondaries are silvery-gray. The Black glides steadily on flat wings. You only see pale feathers at the base of a Black Vulture's fingers.

Eagles

Golden Eagle vs. Bald Eagle. Between the immatures of the Golden and the Bald there is much room for confusion. The immature Bald shows more speckly white in its wing linings. Its dark tail band is not nearly so tidy. In the adult Golden, don't count on seeing any gold. It has a few indistinct whitish bands on its tail, as opposed to one only on the immatures of the Golden and Bald. Eagles glide on flat wings.

---

* Puffins look puffinlike.

Kites

Mississippi Kite vs. Black-shouldered Kite vs. American Swallow-tailed Kite. These have pointy wings. Mississippi: blunt black tail. Black-shouldered: white tail. And black shoulders. Swallow-tailed: swallow tail!

Snail Kite. Rounder wing tips. Dark tail band. Hunts low, like a flappy Northern Harrier, but without the V-wing business.

Harriers

Northern Harrier. White rump. Hunts low, gliding with wings tipped up in a wide V. Overhead, skinny with a long tail.

Accipiters

Accipiters have short, roundish wings and long tails. They spend most of their time dashing through woods after small birds. In migration, they sometimes soar. Characteristic flight is flap, flap, flap, glide; flap, flap, flap, glide. Sexual dimorphism is so pronounced that it is tough to tell a male Cooper's from a female Sharpie. Perched, accipiters tend to lean forward with their backs at a 45-degree angle.

Sharp-shinned Hawk vs. Cooper's Hawk vs. Northern Goshawk. Sharpie has squarish tail. Gliding overhead, it tends to press its wrists forward, ahead of its beak. "Keeps its head in the well." Cooper's has roundish tail. Overhead, it keeps its wings out straight; forms a cross. Goshawk: Big. Big white eyebrow.

Buteos

Soaring hawks inclined to have shortish tails and big round wings. Perched, they sit bolt upright.

Red-shouldered Hawk. Reddish shoulders are somewhat helpful up close, except they are pretty pale in the Southland. Overhead, there is a translucent crescent—a "window"—at the base of the fingers.

Broad-winged Hawk. Flocks numbering in the gazillions are common in migration. Size of a crow.* Otherwise a toughie. Wing has a narrow, darkish trailing edge.

* When you're desperate, a crow up-sun can look eagle-sized.

Red-tailed Hawk. Probably the most common hawk: the one best known for making lazy circles. However, there are subspecies that look entirely unrelated. The red tail is no guarantee. In the East, the belly band is the best mark, but even that isn't always obvious.

Swainson's Hawk. Dark breast in adult plumages. Relatively pointy wings. Wobbles like a Turkey Vulture when soaring.

Rough-legged Hawk. Sometimes hovers. Dark wrists in light phase. Big dark band near end of tail.

Ferruginous Hawk. If the classic Red-tail isn't a Red-tail, try Ferruginous. Look for the legs forming a darker V where they come together at the ankle.

White-tailed Hawk. Clear breast. Dark band on shortish tail.

Common Black-Hawk. Not so common. Could be a Black Vulture except for the white tail-band.

Zone-tailed Hawk. Could be a Turkey Vulture except for the white bands on the tail.

Harris's Hawk. Terrifically two-toney.

Short-tailed Hawk. Short all over for a hawk. Breast and wing linings either all white, or all black.

Osprey. Dark eye stripe. Dark wrists. White breast. Coming at you, its silhouette is like a broad, flattened Golden Arches.

Caracara

Crested Caracara. On the ground, it looks and acts like a giant, killer chicken. In flight, there are big white patches toward the wing tips.

Falcons

Falcons have pointy wings.

American Kestrel. Little, likes to sit on wires. Hovers a lot. Two snazzy sideburns separated by a white cheek.

Merlin. If you see a pigeon that turns into a falcon, it is a Merlin. Bold, dark bands on the tail.

Prairie Falcon. Pale all over, with a darkish armpit. Jet-propelled.

Peregrine Falcon. Many, many subspecies. Dark jowl. Often citified.

Gyrfalcon. Humongous. Looks heavy. Cruises low.

Grouse

Ruffed Grouse vs. Spruce Grouse vs. Blue Grouse vs. Sharp-tailed Grouse vs. Sage Grouse. Ruffed goes off at your feet like a bomb and scares the daylights out of you. Little crest. Darker narrow tail-band. Spruce has dark tail, often with a brownish tip. Blue is not the least bit blue. Dark tail with gray band at tip, except farther north, where it may be bandless. Sharp-tailed has a pointy tail. Sage: big! With a black belly. The one that sounds like popcorn popping.

White-tailed Ptarmigan vs. Rock Ptarmigan vs. Willow Ptarmigan. White-tailed has white outer tail feathers. Rock has black outer tail feathers. Winter male has black smoodge joining its eye and its bill. Willow has black outer tail feathers, but no black smoodge in winter. Ruddier than Rock in summer.

Greater Prairie Chicken vs. Lesser Prairie Chicken. No sweat if you're around in courting time and can check the colors of the neck pouches.

Quail. The only trick with quail is remembering which one says *Chicago* (California), and which one says *Chicago-go* (Gambel's).

Chukar. Boldly barred sides, reddish bill.

Gray Partridge. Reddish-brown face.

Ring-necked Pheasant. Among grousy things, the female Ring-necked is the only one with a long tail and white bags under its eyes.

Pigeons and Doves

Band-tailed Pigeon vs. Red-billed Pigeon vs. White-crowned Pigeon. Band-tailed has skinny white collar at the back. Red-billed is dark all over. White-crowned: white crown.

Rock Dove: "I say it's a pigeon and I say the hell with it."—John James Audubon

Mourning Dove vs. White-winged Dove vs. White-tipped Dove. MoDo can look like damned-near anything in the right light. Long tail. White-winged has splashes of white in its wings. Roundish tail. White-tipped is chubby. White tips on outer tail feathers.

Common Ground Dove vs. Inca Dove. Barring on the Inca's belly.

Cuckoos and Anis

Smooth-billed Ani vs. Groove-billed Ani. Birds that turn out not to be big grackles. The best field mark is geography.

Yellow-billed Cuckoo vs. Black-billed Cuckoo. Go with the undertail. You should be so lucky as to see it. The Yellow-billed's is black and white, Black-billed's gray and white.

Owls

Owls sit upright. The only easy way to find owls is to listen for crows and go see what they're mobbing.

Barn Owl. The only owl, apart from Snowy, with a white face.

Short-eared Owl. No ears to speak of. Round face. Hunts by daylight, early and late. Flaps around like a fluffy butterfly.

Long-eared Owl. Very skinny.

Great Horned Owl. Great. Horned.

Great Gray Owl. Great. No horns.

Barred Owl vs. Spotted Owl. Only Barred in East. Rare in West. But then, so is Spotted. Barred has vertical bars on breast. Spotted has spots. Both have solid black eyes.

Eastern Screech Owl vs. Western Screech Owl vs. Whiskered Screech Owl. Screech owls are little. And their plumage varies like crazy. Apart from that, it's geography.

Flammulated Owl. Eyes all dark. Teeny ears.

Elf Owl. Kind of dull,

Ferruginous Pygmy-Owl vs. Northern Pygmy-Owl. Northern has whitish bars on its tail.

Northern Saw-whet Owl. Rusty. Look for the white paint under the roost.

Northern Hawk Owl. Long tail. Thickly barred from neck down. Likes the daytime. Leans forward on its perch, like an accipiter.

Nightjars

If you hope to spot a nightjar by waiting to see one fly up and suck a goat, forget it. They're much too clever to be caught by the likes of you. Otherwise, this is fertile territory for bird-listeners.

Chuck-will's-widow vs. Whip-poor-will vs. Common Poorwill. Chuck has buffy chin, thin whitish necklace. Whipper has dark chin, whitish necklace. Poorwill has darkish chin with wide, white necklace.

Pauraque. Long roundish tail, whitish nighthawky smudges at base of fingers.

Common Nighthawk vs. Lesser Nighthawk. The forking in their tails is all but invisible. But everybody else's tail is round. Common is fluttery, Lesser is more fluttery. Does that help? Lesser's wing bars don't go all the way across the wing. That won't help much either.

Swifts

Chimney Swift vs. Vaux's Swift. Stumpy tails. Chimney soars more. Chimney is eastern, Vaux's is western. Tough call where they overlap.

Black Swift vs. White-throated Swift. Forked tails. Black is all black.

Hummingbirds

Half the North American hummingbirds don't travel much north of the Mexican border and I'm leaving them to the experts. Female hummers sometimes show a vague hint of the male's chin markings—his "gorget"—but sensible persons do not pin their hopes on this. Sensible persons ignore females.

Ruby-throated Hummingbird. The only hummingbird that regularly lives in the East.

Black-chinned Hummingbird. If you are in the West and think you see a Ruby-throat, check Black-chinned.

Costa's Hummingbird. Head and gorget purple.

Anna's Hummingbird. Head and gorget red. Short-billed, for a hummer.

Calliope Hummingbird. Streaky reddy, purply gorget.

Broad-tailed Hummingbird. If this was the first hummingbird anybody ever saw, they wouldn't be called "hummingbirds," they would be called "whistlingbirds."

Rufous Hummingbird. Rufousy. Wings make a buzzy whistle. Sometimes travels East in the fall.

Allen's Hummingbird. Male has green back. Otherwise, it could be a Rufous.

Kingfishers*

Belted Kingfisher vs. Ringed Kingfisher. Female Belted has rufous belly band. Male and female Ringed have bellies that are *all* rufous.

Green Kingfisher. Weeny. Don't count on it looking green in poor light.

Woodpeckers

Woodpeckers aren't exactly tame, but your presence doesn't much matter to them. Males and females look much alike, but males generally have some, or more, red on their heads. Except for the Three-toed and the Black-backed. Those males have yellow on their heads.

Golden-fronted Woodpecker. Not much gold on its front. Which is its forehead, remember? More on its nape.

Red-bellied Woodpecker. Not much red on belly. Female's red nape goes over the top on the male.

Gila Woodpecker. If Golden-fronted had no gold, and if Red-bellied's only red was a cap on the male.

Northern Flicker. A ground-pecker. Big white rump. You can worry about shaftedness all you like, but it won't do your list any good.

Red-headed Woodpecker. Apart from Red-breasted Sapsucker, the only woodpecker with a head that is all red. Only one with red head and white breast.

Acorn Woodpecker. You could say it is the only black-backed wood-pecker with white at the base of the primaries that doesn't have a white crown. And there is that business with the acorns.

White-headed Woodpecker. Only woodpecker with white crown.

Lewis's Woodpecker. If a crow turns out to be a woodpecker, it is a Lewis's. Also flycatches. Also doesn't have swoopy woodpecker flight. Doesn't much peck wood. Has a thing for acorns.

A Sapsucker Interlude

Sapsuckers all show big white wing patches when perched, or what-ever the hell you call it, up against a tree.

---

* Valuable kingfisher fact: Toe number three and toe number four are joined together.

Williamson's Sapsucker vs. Red-breasted Sapsucker vs. Yellow-bellied Sapsucker. Williamson's male has black crown. Female has brown head. Red-breasted has red head. Yellow-bellied isn't always very yellow-bellied. Red forehead.

Now back to Woodpeckers

Downy Woodpecker vs. Hairy Woodpecker. Downy has wispy little bill. Hairy has whacking big bill.

Three-toed Woodpecker vs. Black-backed Woodpecker. Three-toed has black and white stripes on back. Black-backed is black-backed.

Ladder-backed Woodpecker vs. Nuttall's Woodpecker. Ladder-backed has white cheek with black outline. Nuttall's has black cheek.

Red-cockaded Woodpecker. Forget the cockade. Go for the big white cheek.

Strickland's Woodpecker. Black back, belly all over black spots.

Pileated Woodpecker vs. Ivory-billed Woodpecker. Check bill color.

Flycatchers

Flycatchers sit erect. They have excellent posture. They fly out, catch a fly, then land. Often, when they catch a fly, you can hear their beaks slam shut. Snap! If you're dead set on identifying flycatchers, a lot of them will drive you nuts.

Tyrant Flycatchers

So called because, as flycatchers go, they are big mothers.

Eastern Kingbird. Also at home in the West. Black above, white below, distinct white band at the end of its tail.

Gray Kingbird. Paler, larger, no tail band.

Thick-billed Kingbird. Great big bill. Yellowish belly gets yellower in fall.

Western Kingbird vs. Cassin's Kingbird vs. Tropical Kingbird vs. Couch's Kingbird. Ho ho ho. Check out the tail patterns in the National Geographic. Ho ho ho. Maybe the map will help.

Scissor-tailed Flycatcher. You won't be paying attention. You will think it was just a bird dragging something long and fluttery. You will miss it.

Sulphur-bellied Flycatcher. The only stripy flycatcher.

Great Crested Flycatcher vs. Brown-crested Flycatcher vs. Ash-throated Flycatcher vs. Dusky-capped Flycatcher. See Western Kingbird et al. above? Ho ho ho.

Greater Pewee. Big and dark. Hope for a call: *José Maria*.

Olive-sided Flycatcher. Don't bank on the white fluffs on the lower back. Look for a tweedy sports coat left unbuttoned. Look for a bird perching at the tippity-top of a tall dead branch.

Eastern Wood Pewee vs. Western Wood Pewee. Pewees have wing bars but *no* eye-ring. A good place for the geography dodge.

Eastern Phoebe vs. Black Phoebe vs. Say's Phoebe. Phoebes pump their tails. Eastern has no wing bars *and* no eye-ring. Black very boldly black with white belly. Say's has warm brown tummy.

Vermilion Flycatcher. Females can be tough. Check the mask.

Empidonax Flycatchers

All have wing bars, all have eye-rings, more or less. Beyond that, it's in the ear of the beholder.

Ho ho ho ho ho.

Northern Beardless-Tyrannulet. Hurrying right along . . .

Larks

Eurasian Skylark. El drabbo. White outer tail feathers, white trailing edge on wings.

Horned Lark. Don't count on seeing horns. Black V neck, black cheek, silvery flicker from underwings in flight.

Swallows

Tree Swallow. First swallow north in spring. Only one that winters in United States. Iridescent dark above, clear white below.

Violet-green Swallow. White hips, white around eye.

Purple Martin. Big. Dark or darkish all over.

Bank Swallow. White throat, dirty breast band.

Northern Rough-winged Swallow. Dirty throat.

Cliff Swallow vs. Cave Swallow. Orangy rumps. Cave has buffy throat
and buffy forehead, both. Cliff has dark throat.

Barn Swallow. Only swallow with swallowtail.

Jays, Crows, and Magpies

Everything is pretty clear in the jay department except maybe:

Scrub Jay vs. Gray-breasted Jay. Scrub Jay is wearing a dandyish, but
tasteful, gray-striped ascot. Gray-breasted much duller by comparison.

Clark's Nutcracker. Sometimes looks like a mockingbird, sometimes
acts like a woodpecker.

Mexican Crow. The crow that looks like a standard American Crow at
the Brownsville, Texas, city dump is a Mexican Crow. Soft-spoken.

American Crow. The standard crow.

Northwestern Crow. Looks like the standard crow but is the only
crow along the coast of British Columbia and Alaska.

Fish Crow. Like the standard crow except it sounds as if it is cawing
through a kazoo. (So do juvenile American Crows.)

Common Raven vs. Chihuahuan Raven. Ravens have wedgy tails. Up
close, the Chihuahuan doesn't look as unkempt as the Common. A tough
call.

Wrentit

Wrentit. Blue-gray gnatcatcher shape, all gray.

Titmice and Chickadees and Other Tits

Tufted Titmouse vs. Plain Titmouse. Tufted has rusty sides.

Black-capped Chickadee vs. Carolina Chickadee. A map-reader's de-
light. Unless you can check the DNA, voice is the key.

Mexican Chickadee. Doesn't say *chickadee*.

Mountain Chickadee. White eyebrow.

Chestnut-backed Chickadee. Has chestnut back.

Boreal Chickadee. Sort of browny all over. Sounds like a Black-capped
with a cold.

Siberian Tit. Not a Black-capped, not a Boreal. Betwixt.

Wrentit vs. Bushtit. Both are chickadeeish without the black chin. Wrentit is brown. Bushtit's breast clear gray.

Creepers and Nuthatches

Brown Creeper. Creeps *up* the trunk.

White-breasted Nuthatch vs. Red-breasted Nuthatch vs. Pygmy Nuthatch vs. Brown-headed Nuthatch. White-breasted: white around eye, no eyeline. Red-breasted: black eyeline. Pygmy: sooty cap pulled down below eye. Brown-headed: brown cap pulled below eye.

Wrens

House Wren. The fundamental LBJ. Little brown job.

Winter Wren. A dark Ping-Pong ball with a dicky little tail.

Carolina Wren. Buffy shoulder and below; no white in tail.

Bewick's Wren. Outer tail feathers white with black polka dots.

Marsh Wren vs. Sedge Wren. Some hotshots claim to tell them apart by the length of their bills. In the West, Marsh only. Sedge has whitish streaks on its noggin.

Canyon Wren. White to its breast, chestnut on down.

Rock Wren. Gray back, rusty rump.

Cactus Wren. Too damn big to be a wren. Must be a thrasher or something.

Thrushes

Arctic Warbler.* Water-thrushy eyebrow, but clear breast.

Golden-crowned Kinglet vs. Ruby-crowned Kinglet. Golden-crowned has eyebrow. Ruby-crowned has eye ring.

Blue-gray Gnatcatcher vs. Black-tailed Gnatcatcher. Blue-gray never has a black crown. Underside of tail is white. Black-tailed's tail has black underside.

Eastern Bluebird vs. Western Bluebird vs. Mountain Bluebird. Eastern is red from chin down. Western: a blue (male) or gray (female) bib.

---

* This is the only Old World warbler that breeds in North America. If you ever happen to run into any other Old World warblers, you will understand why you should be grateful.

Mountain: no red at all, except maybe a blush on the female's bazoom after breeding.

Townsend's Solitaire. Wait! That long, skinny flycatcher up there isn't a flycatcher at all.

Varied Thrush. Robiny with orange eyebrow.

American Robin. Overhead against a bright sky it will take you ages to figure out what the hell it is. Until you learn its flap. Merrily it rows along.

Shrikes

Loggerhead Shrike vs. Northern Shrike. If it has a mask, it's not a mockingbird or a Clark's Nutcracker. If it makes a last-instant sharp upswoop to land, it's a shrike. Which one? The books are full of sound advice, but it beats me.

The Spotted Thrushes*

Wood	Veery	Hermit	Swainson's†	Gray-cheeked†
Reddish head, brownish tail	*Reddish head to tail* (a shade darker in the West)‡	Brownish head, *reddish tail—* WHICH IT WAGS!	All dark back (except in the West, where it's reddy)‡	All dark back
Big bold spots	Faint spots (except in the West, where they're dark)	Average spots	Average spots (except in the West, where they're faint)	Average spots

* This is easier than it looks.§

† Swainson's and Gray-cheeked look alike in most lights. The key is Swainson's outstanding eye-ring.

‡ Veery and Swainson's virtually switch their eastern costumes in the West. The key again is Swainson's eye-ring.

§ No, it's not.

Mimic Thrushes

Repetition Rule: If it says things only once, it is a Gray Catbird; if it repeats things two or three times, it is a thrasher of some sort; if it repeats things over and over and over and over, it is a Northern Mockingbird. Interesting that *the* bird of the South is called Northern, eh?

Sage Thrasher. Kind of gray. Most of the tail tip is white. Too dark to be a juvenile mocker, and not very thrashery in manner.

Brown Thrasher vs. Long-billed Thrasher. Brown is eastern. It is way too big to be a spotted thrush, and its spots are too stripy. The Long-billed is an overstated Brown with an orange eye.

Curve-billed Thrasher vs. Bendire's Thrasher. These have speckly breasts. Curve-billed has curvier bill.

Crissal Thrasher vs. Le Conte's Thrasher vs. California Thrasher. These have clear breasts. Le Conte's is very pale everywhere. Crissal vs. California is a problem. Crissal's undertail coverts are more like a catbird's; California has a whitish eyebrow.

Pipits and Wagtails

When you look at the illustrations, there is something about the slimness and streamlining of these birds that makes you expect something much bigger. They are teentsy. "Sparrow-sized," as the big shooters say.

American Pipit vs. Sprague's Pipit vs. Red-throated Pipit. The American (formerly Water Pipit) shows up all over the place; has the plainest back. Sprague's: clear, buffy cheek. Mottled back. Red-throated: really stripy back.

Waxwings

Bohemian Waxwing vs. Cedar Waxwing. Bohemian has rusty undertail coverts and yellow in wing tips. Cedar doesn't.

Starlings

European Starling. Juvenile is all gray, with none of standard marks. Has adult's lousy posture.

Vireos

Vireos vs. Warblers. With time, you will see that vireos have more businesslike bills, with little hooks at the tip of the upper. That warblers are terribly flighty and never sit still; vireos move with a much more stately grace.*

There are two sorts of vireos: (1) the sort with spectacles and wing bars, and (2) the sort with eye stripes and no wing bars. Within the groups, what sets them apart is the degree of yellow, and where it is.

Number 1. Spectacles and Wing bars. Black-capped Vireo vs. Solitary Vireo. They look as if they're wearing little football helmets. Black-capped's helmet is blacker than Solitary's. Rocky Mountain Solitary has almost no yellow.

White-eyed Vireo. Only spectacled vireo with light irises.

Yellow-throated Vireo. Yellow specs, yellow throat.

Bell's Vireo vs. Hutton's Vireo. You got problems. Hutton's seems to be wearing half-moon reading glasses; no rim at top.

Gray Vireo. All gray. The Solitary in the Rockies has bolder spectacles.

Number 2. Eye stripes and No Wing bars. Red-eyed Vireo. Very dark stripe through eye, very black eyebrow.

Black-whiskered Vireo. Same as above, plus whisker.

Warbling Vireo vs. Philadelphia Vireo. Easier in East since eastern Warbling has almost no yellow. Mind you, the Philadelphia's yellow can be anything from bright to almost nonexistent. In the West: geography.

Warblers

The trouble with warblers is infinite, including a crippling physical ailment† for the birder. Peterson is the best for organizing warblers into groupings with similar field marks. This, however, has nothing to do with biology. His "Confusing Fall Warblers" pages are immensely comforting at the outset.

My advice is, as ever: Take it easy. Proceed slowly. For the first little while, satisfy yourself with breeding males. Some females are obviously

---

* Or they are dozier, one or the other.

† Warbler Neck. See under Diseases.

related to the males, so try them next. The warblers that nest in your bailiwick might tempt you to try some juveniles at a more leisurely clip. Then comes fall migration and all hell breaks loose because many warblers become masters of disguise.

Among confusing males: Only these make really significant costume changes after breeding: Tennessee, Chestnut-sided, Cape May, Magnolia, Yellow-rumped, Bay-breasted, Blackpoll, and Palm. All the others keep some trace of their breeding marks.

Warblers that *warble:* Yellow-rumped, Canada, Painted Redstart.

Warblers that *wag* their tails. Or pump their tails. Whatever: Palm, Prairie, Kirtland's.

Warblers that *twitch* their tails: Virginia's, Lucy's, Blackburnian, Black-throated Green.

Warblers that *spread* their tails: Hooded, Magnolia, American Redstart, Painted Redstart.

Warblers frequently seen *walking* on the ground: Ovenbird, Northern Waterthrush, Louisiana Waterthrush, Connecticut (Mourning and Mac-Gillivray's *hop*), Swainson's, Kentucky. The Worm-eating likes brush piles and clusters of dead leaves.

Warblers that regularly *flycatch:* American Redstart, Painted Redstart, Wilson's, Canada.

Warbler with *no characteristics and no field marks of any sort:* Orange-crowned.

Hybrids. A number of warbler groups seem to have broken up into species fairly recently, and affectionate bonds remain. Blue-winged and Golden-winged, the best known, produce two basic hybrids. These don't count on your checklist, so the hell with them.* However, all sorts of other species screw other species as they come along and might produce fertile offspring. These tend to disappear back into the uniformity mill fairly quickly. Some affinity groups are obvious: Connecticut, Mourning, and MacGillivray's. Some cross the line so freely that the line disappears—Audubon's and Myrtle are now but one: Yellow-rumped.

---

* If you want to look up their pictures in the field guides, go ahead. It won't make any difference.

Blue-winged Warbler vs. Golden-winged Warbler. Golden-winged has yellow wing bars; a dark—to black—chin and throat. Blue-winged has sharp, black eye stripe.

Tennessee Warbler. Brightish eyebrow, darkish eye stripe.

Orange-crowned Warbler. Seeing the orange crown is a one-in-a-million shot. Otherwise, no field marks.*

Bachman's Warbler. Yellow forehead. Male has black throat.

Nashville Warbler. White eye-ring, brightish yellow from chin down.

Virginia's Warbler. Yellow smudge on breast, yellow undertail coverts.

Lucy's Warbler. Rusty rump.

Northern Parula. Eye-ring divided across middle. Male has a rainbow across chest.

Black-and-White Warbler. Climbs tree trunks. Two broad black stripes on head.

Black-throated Blue Warbler. Always, the white pocket handkerchief.

Chestnut-sided Warbler. Lime-green topsides in fall.

Cerulean Warbler. Male has dark necklace. Female quite green on back and crown.

Cape May Warbler. The pale—sometimes paler than others—spot where shoulder meets neck.

Magnolia Warbler vs. Yellow-rumped Warbler. Both have yellow rumps. Magnolia always has a yellow breast. Yellow-rumped has yellow on sides.

The next five have the same fashion designer.

1. Black-throated Gray Warbler. Only yellow is a dab between eyeball and corner of bill.

2. Townsend's Warbler. Black cheek bordered by yellow.

3. Hermit Warbler. Sides of face clear yellow.

4. Black-throated Green Warbler. The only easterner. Smudgy line through eye.

---

* Sounds kind of ineffable, this business of no field marks. In fact, identifying an Orange-crowned can be as effable as birding gets.

5. Golden-cheeked Warbler. Line through eye extends back to dark haircut.

Yellow-throated Warbler vs. Grace's Warbler. Yellow-throated has white behind its ears and a white eyebrow. Grace's has yellow eyebrow that turns white behind the eye.

Kirtland's Warbler. Prairie Warbler with split eye-ring, gray face.

Prairie Warbler. Yellow eyebrow, black stripes on sides.

Bay-breasted Warbler vs. Blackpoll Warbler. No problem in breeding. (Male Blackpoll has solid black crown; Black-and-White has black stripes.) Fall males are a bastard. Blackpoll has pale legs.

Pine Warbler. Blah, but not as blah as an Orange-crowned. Has wing bars, pale undertail.

Palm Warbler. Rusty cap. Western birds are altogether paler in the fall.

Yellow Warbler. Almost always, there is some hint of rusty chest streaks. Beady eye.

Mourning Warbler vs. MacGillivray's Warbler vs. Connecticut Warbler. Mourning has no eye-ring to speak of. MacGillivray's eye-ring is broken in half. Connecticut's eye-ring is visible from space.

Kentucky Warbler. Just as you are about to say, "Holy gazonga, a Hooded!" you see it isn't completely hooded. Great sideburns.

Canada Warbler. Just as you are about to say, "Holy gazonga, a Kentucky!" you see the necklace.

Hooded Warbler. "Holy gazonga, a Hooded!" Spreads tail, showing a lot of white.

Wilson's Warbler. Yarmulke. Underside of tail feathers black.

Worm-eating Warbler vs. Swainson's Warbler. Worm-eating* has stripy head. Swainson's is duller, un-stripy.

Louisiana Waterthrush vs. Northern Waterthrush. Louisiana has more *flare* to its eyebrows, pinky legs.

Common Yellowthroat. She has gray face, yellow throat. As warblers go, Rubenesque.

---

* Not even W. C. Fields could bring himself to say, "Well, my little Worm-eating Warbler . . ."

Grosbeaks, Buntings, and Sparrows

Toward the end of the passerines, and the ends of the field guides themselves, all the books get kind of rambly. The National Geographic interrupts its finches and finchy birds with a digression into blackbirds and on through the tanagers—into which they throw the meadowlarks and a bunch of other junk. Then back to finchy matters. Nobody puts all the grosbeaks together. I'm still mainly following the National Geographic, but don't expect it to make terrific sense.

Rose-breasted Grosbeak. Female very stripy, with white eyebrow.

Black-headed Grosbeak. Yellow wing linings. Female buffier than Rose-breasted; not stripy.

Pyrrhuloxia. That cardinal-looking thing has a big yellow bill.

Blue Grosbeak. Female should be called Brown Grosbeak. Little blue shoulder flash. Flicks tail.

Indigo Bunting vs. Lazuli Bunting. Indigo male gets ratty after breeding. Female very gray. Lazuli female buffy below.

Painted Bunting vs. Varied Bunting. Painted female is almost as green as grass. Juveniles are various shades of green. Varied female is brown.

Towhees

Green-tailed Towhee. White throat.

Eastern Towhee. Used to be the eastern Rufous-sided. Female has brown back, brown head.

Spotted Towhee. Formerly western Rufous-sided. Spots in question are white ones, on the back.

Brown Towhee vs. Albert's Towhee. Albert's has a black mask.

Sparrows

The tenth circle of Hell. Damn near all of them have white throats. The sexes are pretty much the same, if that is any consolation.

Grasshopper Sparrow. Does not exist. Mythical. A product of The Big Lie.

Baird's Sparrow. Buffy face. Rusty-yellow crown stripe.

Henslow's Sparrow. Greeny face and back of the neck.

Le Conte's Sparrow. Orangy eyebrow, white crown stripe.

Nelson's Sharp-tailed Sparrow. Northerner split from what used to be the Sharp-tailed Sparrow. Orangy eyebrow, gray crown stripe.

Salt-marsh Sharp-tailed Sparrow. The southerner. Side of face notably orange.

Seaside Sparrow. Many, many, many versions. Yellow spot between eye and bill.

Vesper Sparrow. White outer tail feathers. Buff shoulders.

Savannah Sparrow. Variations to burn. Look for something yellowish in the face, especially eyebrows.

Song Sparrow. There are as many as thirty-one identifiably different races of the Song Sparrow. And you probably thought it would be one of the easy ones. Tail-pumper in flight. Round tail. Don't count on a breast spot.

Lark Sparrow. Wearing a lot of makeup for a sparrow. Big white tail tips.

Black-throated Sparrow. White eyebrows, too.

Five-striped Sparrow. Dark spot on gray breast.*

Sage Sparrow. Dark spot on whitish breast. Sometimes, stripish breast. Sleek gray head on the Pacific coast.

Bachman's Sparrow. Damned if I know.

Botteri's Sparrow vs. Cassin's Sparrow. National Geographic says Botteri's is "a large, plain sparrow" and Cassin's is "a large, drab sparrow." You're on your own from there.

Rufous-winged Sparrow. Two whisker stripes.

Rufous-crowned Sparrow. One whisker stripe.

American Tree Sparrow. "The winter Chippie": if the Chipping Sparrow didn't go all to hell and lose its rufous headgear in winter, it would look like a Tree Sparrow. Only the Tree has that black chest spot.

Field Sparrow. Pink bill.

Chipping Sparrow. In breeding, the eyebrow is a bolt of white lightning. In winter, there is something rusty about the stripy crown.

Clay-colored Sparrow. As if the Lark Sparrow didn't put on its makeup.

Brewer's Sparrow. Amid the drabness, a white eye ring.

Black-chinned Sparrow. Gray bird with brown wings.

---

* In case you're too busy to count the stripes.

Juncos

Dark-eyed Junco vs. Yellow-eyed Junco. Dark-eyed is depressingly variable. But it always has a dark eye. Adult Yellow-eyed has a yellow eye.

My God! It's back to *SPARROWS*.

Harris's Sparrow. That House Sparrow sure is huge. Then you see it has a black crown.

White-throated Sparrow. Be careful; some have buffy instead of white stripes on their heads.

White-crowned Sparrow. Juvenile is beige-crowned.

Golden-crowned. It might not be much, but the gold's always there.

Fox Sparrow. Big sparrow. Big markings.

Lincoln's Sparrow. Buffy chest band, fine streaks, gray face.

Swamp Sparrow. Rusty wings.

Longspurs

Chestnut-collared Longspur vs. McCown's Longspur vs. Smith's Longspur vs. Lapland Longspur. In the East it is probably a Lapland. Breeding plumages are distinctive, but winter, oog! In winter, Chestnut-collared male shows blackish breast, McCown's male shows a blackish bib, Smith's male is very buffy from chin to butt, and Lapland has stripy flanks.

Snow Bunting vs. McKay's Bunting. Male Snow has black back; other Snow backs are dark. Male McKay's has a white back; other McKay's backs are pale.

Dickcissel. There seems to be a lot of yellow on that House Sparrow.

Lark Bunting. The big wing patch.

Blackbirds and Orioles

Bobolink. Breeding male has "a dress suit on backward"—Peterson. Female and winter males: very buffy, with striped crown.

Eastern Meadowlark vs. Western Meadowlark. They have the Starling's lousy hunched posture. The Eastern doesn't sing so great. The Western is a regular Pavarotti.

Yellow-headed Blackbird. Somewhere there is some yellow.

Red-winged Blackbird. *Nothing* else is as stripy as the female.

Tricolored blackbird. The hem of the red patch is white. On the Red-winged it is yellowish.

Rusty Blackbird vs. Brewer's Blackbird. Breeding male Rusty is plain black. Breeding male Brewer's has purplish iridescence. Rusty male turns very rusty after breeding. Some Brewer's males get mildly rusty, but mostly they don't. Rusty female has a dark eye. Brewer's female's is yellow.

Brown-headed Cowbird vs. Bronzed Cowbird. Male Bronzed has a red eye. Female Bronzed is black; female Brown-headed is lavender gray.

Common Grackle vs. Boat-tailed Grackle vs. Great-tailed Grackle. Common can have purple sheen, can have bronze sheen. Boat-tailed and Great-tailed females are brown birds. Where Boat-tails and Great-tails overlap, Boat-tails have dark eyes. On the Atlantic Coast it has yellow eyes. Who worked this out?

Orioles

Scott's Oriole. Yellow version of Baltimore. Female has darkish head.

Orchard Oriole. Strikingly dark. Female is yellow, with a light head.

Baltimore Oriole. Retrieved from the lumpers. Hooray! No longer part of the Northern Oriole stew but its own bird. Striking black hood. Easterner.

Bullock's Oriole. Was lumped with Baltimore, now unlumped. Orange face. White wing flash. Westerner.

Hooded Oriole vs. Altamira Oriole. Why is Hooded called Hooded? Good question. Altamira is a wide-screen version with an orange epaulette.

Spot-breasted Oriole. Has spots on its breast.

Tanagers

Scarlet Tanager vs. Western Tanager. Scarlets have big yellow bills, which is how you know the females and fall males aren't giant warblers. The Scarlet male has black wings in all plumages. The Western has black wings with wing bars.

Summer Tanager vs. Hepatic Tanager. Males have reddish-black wings. Hepatics have grayish cheek patches.

Weavers

House Sparrow. Just when you think you know what you're doing, the female will make you look like an idiot.

Finches

Pine Siskin. That Goldfinch looks awfully stripy.

American Goldfinch vs. Lesser Goldfinch vs. Lawrence's Goldfinch. American in winter keeps dark wings, has white undertail coverts. Lesser has yellow undertail coverts. The female Lawrence's is a gray bird with a yellow wash on the chest.

Red Crossbill vs. White-winged Crossbill. White-winged has wing bars, Red doesn't.

Pine Grosbeak. Red or yellowish head. Big dark bill.

Common Redpoll vs. Hoary Redpoll. Common is not so hoary as the Hoary. The more you stare at Commons,* the Hoarier they look.

Rosy Finch. Pinky wings.

Purple Finch vs. Cassin's Finch vs. House Finch. Male Purple has no brown stripes on its sides; female has big white eyebrow. Male Cassin's has a sort of red cap, female paler than House female. House male has dark stripes on its sides and breast.

Evening Grosbeak. Big pale bill. Big white wing patches. For you Michigan Wolverines fans, the male is wearing their football helmet.

* A symptom of Twitchy Lister Finger. See under Diseases.

Part 6

The Ten North American Hotspots a Birder Absolutely Has to See Before Dying

a Story: I met a birder who was leaving for Cuba. He was on his way into the forested interior where the Ivory-billed Woodpecker had most recently, and reliably, been seen. The political situation in Cuba was tense; tourists had been cautioned to step carefully. I asked how he would feel if he was massacred by restless Cubans, but in the instant before the machete whacked him in two, he'd had an Ivory-billed Woodpecker in his binoculars.

His reply: "I'd say it had been a pretty good day."

It is possible to have a pretty good day at every one of the places listed here. Some of the suggestions will seem a bit narrow. For instance, the first is Aransas, and unless you live in the neighborhood, anybody who goes to Aransas might as well consider doing the whole schmear: swing west along the Gulf Coast and up the Rio Grande, hitting the traditional stops: Laguna Atascosa, the King Ranch, the Brownsville Dump, Bentsen State Park, Santa Ana, Falcon Dam. You have entered the realm of the deranged at this stage, but you can do it in a week. Then there is southern Florida. Where to begin, where to end, where to draw the line? I have drawn the line this way: at the right time of year,* you can get your rocks off with a one-day shot at each of these places.

The ranking is alphabetical.

* Even at the wrong time of year. As General De Gaulle said about French wine, when it is good it is excellent, and when it's not good it is still pretty good.

Aransas, Texas

For the Whooping Cranes. They're here from about the beginning of December to the end of May. There are lots of other things to see: almost 270 birds on the list. And no end of habitat: more than fifty thousand acres of meadowland, prairie, dunes, tide marshes, windswept bay. Aransas was created to protect the Whoopers, and they seem to appreciate it, since they keep coming back. You can see them from the landward side, but you can't get very close. To get familiar, you have to go out on one of the local charters that cruise the intercoastal waterway. The skippers know the birds by name, their family background, and whether they are creatures of substance or fly-by-nighters, and nudge you right in to meet them. If you ever want a spooky sense of a bird's vulnerability, this skinny bit of shore where the hurricanes prowl and the oil platforms line the horizon will make the hair on the back of your neck stand up. The nearest town with much by way of accommodation is Rockport. You can get well fed in Rockport, but if you are not utterly opposed to hanging out, it is the barrooms that have a particular allure.

Caution: The men, and the women, who are the locals, have seen more western movies than is good for them and are inclined to behave as if they are in one. Anybody wearing anything from L. L. Bean is advised to sit with their back to the wall and mind their manners.

Aransas National Wildlife Refuge
PO Box 100
Austwell, TX 77950

Cape May, New Jersey

F. Scott Fitzgerald said three-quarters of New Jersey is under water, and the rest is under surveillance. If he was talking about bird surveillance, he had Cape May in mind. It squeezes just about everything that scoots south down the Atlantic Coast into a splendid funnel between Delaware Bay and the deep blue sea, pouring it out right there, before your eyes. There are four noteworthy locations. The Cape May Bird Observatory, with its hawk-watching platform. The William D. and Vane C. Blair Migratory Bird Refuge. Higbee Beach Wildlife Management Area. And, up the highway a bit, toward Atlantic City, Stone Harbor, with its wading-bird rookery, where a gazillion herons and egrets coming home to roost bucking the traffic of a gazillion night herons flying out is a sunset sight that will knock you on your keister. There are more than 320 species on the Cape May list, but the big noise is the fall hawk migration that the Audubon Society tracks at the observatory in the state park. There are other places to overdose on hawks (Hawk Mountain in Pennsylvania is probably the best known), but no place that offers as much other stuff. And definitely no place that offers the gourmet wonders of Cape May; it is about as hard to get a bad meal there as it is in Paris. In New Jersey. Who knew? The Victorian architecture is its own distraction.

Cape May Bird Observatory
New Jersey Audubon Society
PO Box 3
Cape May, NJ 08212

Cheyenne Bottoms, Kansas

When migrating Whooping Cranes stop over, Sandhill Crane hunting is suspended. If it is beyond your immediate comprehension that anyone would ever feel the need to shoot Sandhill Cranes, you have to consider that they constitute a local pest. Twelve thousand of them at a time mooching around the ponds and wetlands is not uncommon. The day's-end arrival of twelve thousand of anything is worth a trip anywhere, and if they are Sandhill Cranes, it's even worth a trip to Kansas, as unlikely a birding spot as most people can imagine. At first. But ask the shorebirds and waterfowl that use Cheyenne Bottoms as Grand Central Station; it is about the busiest staging area for shorebirds on the continent. Like many refuges run by states, and by provinces in Canada, hunting seems to be the number-one reason for Cheyenne Bottoms's existence, and will probably remain so until governments figure out a way to sell bird-watching licenses. So steel yourself for the sight of an awful lot of duck blinds. The nearest town with accommodation is Great Bend, nobody's idea of a vacation paradise. And prairie cooking is prairie cooking (watch out for the oysters). But keep these opinions to yourself and the folks will treat you nice.

Cheyenne Bottoms
Box 301
Great Bend, KS 67530

Churchill, Manitoba

It's a long way from anywhere, almost impossible to get to, and the mosquitoes can bite through the bottom of a snowmobile boot. Florida brags about its mosquitoes. Forget it. If Florida wants to call those things mosquitoes, Churchill is plagued by swarms of bloodsucking Boeing 747s. Birders get so dribbly at the thought of going to Churchill that Hudson Bay might be the torrid Mediterranean for all they're concerned. Next to the mosquitoes, the polar bears are hardly worth bothering about. Ross's Gull, which evolution for some reason made pink, and pinker in the mood for love, is the star of the show. Short of the ends of the earth, Churchill is the nearest place you can find it nesting. There isn't a big local list, but the regulars insist every bird is a quality bird, particularly the Arctic species. Species converge because there is a convergence of habitat: tundra, taiga, boreal forest, ice floes. From Cape Merry, you can watch the whales. And you can bird your brains out; the summer sun shines from three in the morning until just shy of midnight. Trouble is, summer only lasts for two days. There's no road in, you fly or go by train. Since the town's continuing existence depends on the whim—and it is very whimsical—of the Canadian grain-shipment subsidization policy (too long a story to go into, but utterly riveting), even regular rail and air access could suddenly disappear. There aren't many places to stay, and you want to book a rental car well ahead. Did I mention the blackflies?

Northern Resource Development Centre
PO Box 760
Churchill, Manitoba RoB oEo

Ding Darling and Corkscrew Swamp, Florida

A combo, easily done in a day. Easily done every day. Somewhere between the flights of Roseate Spoonbills into Ding and the courtship flights of Swallow-tailed Kites over Corkscrew, you discover what mainlining is all about. J. N. "Ding" Darling, a nature cartoonist and early conservation activist, created, among other things, this preserve on Sanibel and the Aransas preserve for Whooping Cranes. Ding's glory— Ding the refuge, that is—is the five-mile drive among tide pools and through mangrove swamp. This is birding at its most leisurely; you can keep the air conditioner on. The joint starts jumping when the tide goes out and the mudflats pull flocks out of the sky. If this coincides with cocktail hour and you happen to have a Thermos of Margaritas handy, life gets so close to perfect you're liable to wade out and dance with the Reddish Egrets. You won't even notice the no-see-ums. Hardly, anyway.

Corkscrew is forty minutes inland. It is freshwater ponds and cypress swamp; one of the few virgin stands of bald cypress left. The world's greatest boardwalk leads to trees full of nesting Wood Storks, as goofy a sight as nature allows. The cries of Limpkins raise the dead. The woods are thick with local birds all year and crawling with migrants spring and fall. Because Corkscrew operates on bankers' hours, it is no problem to cruise Ding at dawn, take a leisurely crack at Corkscrew (bring lunch, there is nothing to eat for miles), and be back at Ding for the twilight show. Mind you, getting across the Sanibel causeway and negotiating the island's main drag are among the worst traffic tortures on the continent; avoid this when the beach crowd is heading out in the morning and home in the late afternoon. Florida cuisine is swell because you don't need teeth to eat it.

J. N. "Ding" Darling National Wildlife Refuge
1 Wildlife Drive
Sanibel, FL 33957

Corkscrew Swamp Sanctuary
375 Sanctuary Road
Naples, FL 33964

Jamaica Bay, New York

City birding is its own torment, so if you're going to do it, you might as well *do* it and bird the mother of all North American cities. If you don't have the balls to try the Ramble in Central Park—and not all birders see themselves as Sylvester Stallone—Jamaica Bay is a perfect alternative. Between Sandy Hook and Coney Island, under the glide path of the jets landing at JFK, and entirely within the city limits; the towers of Manhattan are ranged behind you. Welcome to Brooklyn. Where else are there nine thousand acres of prime coastal birding you can get to by subway? (The IND train, A or CC, to the Rockaways. Get off at Broad Channel station. Walk west to Cross Bay Boulevard, turn right and go half a mile. Or you could grab a cab.) Ponds and dunes and five miles of trails, not including the ones at Dead Horse Bay on Flatbush Avenue. Since it is part of an enormous recreation area run by the National Parks Service, a program-intensive agency, there is always lots going on. If you ever wondered what "mixed recreational use" meant, anyplace in New York City with a beach is where you can find out. Migration, either way, is the time to be there. Try not to look like a tourist. This is an especially good trick for a bird-watcher with binoculars. New York birders, being New Yorkers, are characteristically modest about Jamaica Bay and figure if you haven't birded there, you don't know nothing about anything.

Jamaica Bay Unit
Gateway National Recreation Area
Floyd Bennett Field
Headquarters Building 69
Brooklyn, NY 11234

Point Pelee, Ontario

It is too damned crowded. The biggest favor you can do yourself and other serious birders is to tell everybody you meet who is just getting interested in birding that Point Pelee is a complete dumper, that the stories about it are all crap, and they would do far better to find themselves a quiet sewage lagoon in someplace like Cleveland and forget the whole thing. In other words, lie. If you don't, you will end up boogacity when the spring warblers are lighting the park up like a pinball machine that has gone nuclear. (Forty-one warbler species recorded, including Kirtland's.) A six-mile spit of dunes and marsh and Carolinian woods sticking like an eyelash into Lake Erie, Pelee, when a migration wave is running, will leave your jeans creamed for life. They have a name for one-hundred-species days in the first weeks of May. They are known as "slow days." Except, on the days when there aren't any birds around, which makes everybody crazy, and with the mobs that show up now, you have to wait in line for a tree you can bang your head against. Southern birds overshooting their breeding grounds make Pelee an even bigger draw: Worm-eating Warbler, ibises, Summer Tanager, Purple Gallinule, Scissor-tailed Flycatcher. Unless your family has been renting a motel room for the last three generations, it is almost impossible to find a nearby place to stay when the crunch is on, and the local food will never replace Mother's even if Mother thought a gourmet dinner meant Spam.

Point Pelee National Park
RR 1
Leamington, Ontario N8H 3V4

Ramsey Canyon, Arizona

Don't take my word for it. Roger Tory Peterson says there are more nesting land birds in southeastern Arizona than in any comparable area of the United States. Why, then, given Arizona's choices, Ramsey Canyon? The Elegant Trogon is one reason. Fourteen species of hummingbird is another. It is the best place for hummingbirds in Arizona, which makes it the best place in the United States. The overall list is smallish, only 150 species, but Ramsey Canyon is smallish, only three hundred acres. That's a pretty good ratio of birds to landscape. If you go all this way and don't see a trogon, it is not only understandable that you would want to end it all, but very easy to do since this particular landscape is a mile above sea level and, being deep in the Huachucas Mountains, most of it is vertical. If faraway fields sometimes look greener, from here you can spit into Mexico, where fifty-one species of hummingbirds have been recorded.

Accommodation is extremely limited, and only a restricted number of people are allowed to wander on the trails at any given time, so plan ahead. Down the mountains, all is Sonoran Desert with Cactus Wrens and roadrunners. If your tastes run to Tex-Mex, you will grow fat and happy down here as long as you remember that no one in an Arizona bar is particularly interested in your political views, even if they ask you directly. Best you just be a good listener.

Ramsey Canyon Preserve

27 Ramsey Canyon Road

Hereford, AZ 85615

Salton Sea, California

Speaking of sewage lagoons, there hasn't been one so far. This isn't one, either, except that it is sort of nature's own. The smell is just as fine, maybe finer. Anciently, the Gulf of California flowed up into these valleys, only to be cut off and left to evaporate, which it did, into an alkali hell called the Salton Sink. The Colorado River, diverted to turn the Imperial Valley green, flooded in 1905 and burst the irrigation levees, filling the Salton Sink. Presto! Now it is the Salton Sea, 227 feet below sea level, and saltier than the ocean itself. It smells worse as time goes on because all manner of pollutants, including no end of chemical fertilizers, drain into it, and there is still no way out except evaporation. But what makes it truly distinctive is that birds love it. They have combined to give it as wide a variety of species—some 380 recorded—as can be found north of Tijuana.

Something about all these birds in such a horrible place stirs the mind. It's a big sea, thirty-five miles long and as much as fifteen wide, and it takes a bit of exploring, but if you can't think of any other reason to go to California, this is a good one. In California, as everywhere else in the United States, it is best to proceed on the assumption that everyone you meet is heavily armed. The wine is cheap, and you can always flee eighty miles south to San Diego and visit the penguins at the zoo.

Salton Sea National Wildlife Refuge
906 West Sinclair Road
Calipatria, CA 92233

Witless Bay, Newfoundland

I have been accused of picking Witless Bay because of the name. That is ridiculous. There are names like this all over Newfoundland. How about Dildo? I could have picked that. I picked Witless Bay because of the puffins. On days when there is no fog and the sea is calmish,* the toughest part of birding Witless Bay is selecting which of the fiercely competitive, and relentlessly colorful, local charter-boat captains to sail with. Working out of Witless Bay and Bay Bulls, they tootle around three islands, Gull, Green, and Great, to give you a gander at what might be the most enormous agglomeration of seabirds in the whole wide world.

Among the most famous of the islands' residents is Leach's Storm-Petrel, and it would be worth the trip just to see it. Except you won't. It leaves before sunup and returns after sundown, and them as aren't certified scientists aren't allowed to step foot on the islands to stumble around among the storm-petrels' nesting burrows. But knowing they're there counts for something, surely. And seeing the puffins can count for just about everything.

Dress warmly; even on the mildest day, a breeze can come up that will leave your brass monkey singing soprano. No one who is not from there has ever had anything good to say about Newfoundland food, and this isn't the place to start. The famous indigenous liquor, however, is another matter. It is called Screech. It is made from owls. Cheers!

Witless Bay Seabird Sanctuary
c/o Parks Division
Department of Tourism, Culture and Recreation
PO Box 8700
St. John's, Newfoundland A1B 4J6

* Some don't be afraid of the sea, and they goes down to the sea, and they be drownded. But I be afraid of the sea, and I goes down to the sea, and I only be drownded now and again.—Old Newfoundland saying

Epilogue

G iven the unique opportunities for some sensational bird-watching, it is surprising how little gets done during midair collisions between birds and aircraft. Since 1983, when North American transportation safety boards started keeping separate files on accidents in which birds were a factor, seventy-seven have been deemed worthy of investigation, but what you get in the reports is seldom of any use to the dedicated lister. Mostly it is "a big bird" did this, "a large bird" whacked that, "a flock of large water birds" went *whump!*

It is rare to encounter such specifics as "three Oldsquaws (ducks) which averaged 1½ pounds each contacted the aircraft," and nice to reflect that the inspector, besides noting that one of the Oldsquaws knocked out 70 percent of the windshield and forced the Cessna 172 to land at Fort Meade, was so sensitive to the needs of his audience that he parenthetically inserted "(ducks)" for those who might otherwise wonder what Oldsquaws* were, and what the hell they were doing eighteen hundred feet over Maryland.

Those of you who have survived the *Down & Dirty* ordeal with birding appetites whetted can only despair, after wading through precise details of lives lost and expensive machinery pranged, at such sloppy observations as "presumed to be a red-tailed hawk" and "thought to be a cormorant." And those of you who rent Alfred Hitchcock's movie *The Birds* to cheer for the feathered friends, will be disappointed to discover how little menace they actually are to human air travelers. Bearing in

* On its own, it can be a loaded term.

mind, of course, that a Snow Goose coming across the dashboard of your Piper Cherokee packs a wallop: imagine getting the Christmas turkey in the kisser at a combined speed of three hundred miles per hour.

While three airliners have been downed temporarily (a Convair 580 with 32 passengers, a Boeing 727 with 64 passengers, and a Boeing 737 with 102 passengers; crew and passengers shaken up at most), in all the accidents taken together, there have only been eleven fatalities, and among those let something be set down for the record:

🐦 One pilot, the autopsy showed, was drunk.

🐦 One, a stunt pilot performing stunts, was not watching where he was going.

🐦 An instructor and a student bought it when the student, seeing "heavy bird activity," yanked the wheel one way, and the instructor yanked it the other, and the student yanked it back his way, and the instructor yanked it back his way, and they yanked it back and forth like this for a while, "which resulted in design limitations of right wing being exceeded."

🐦 And then there was the passenger in a helicopter that went all wobbly after its tail rotor pureed "a large sea bird." Since they were over the Pacific Ocean, the pilot and the passenger discussed the possibility of the passenger, at least, being saved by jumping from the helicopter, *and he did*—"dove out head first"—*and drowned!* After which the pilot brought the chopper down safely.

The point being that birds deserve a lot less credit than myth gives them, and those air passengers who clutch their seatbelts with the ghastly premonition that they will momentarily join all the thousands who have gone to the great baggage claim in the sky after enormous, turbine-clogging flocks of seagulls were hoovered into the Pratt & Whitneys should take a Valium.

So much for birding assuming a practical role in our daily affairs. We will have to make do with its impractical aspects, which have been carefully laid out in these pages. If I have missed any, you are nevertheless perfectly equipped to stumble over them on your own, and before very long.

Here are what birding has given me over the years:

🐦 The joy that goes with doing something that leaves me thoroughly bewildered in circumstances that are almost always unpleasant.

🐦 And probably some other things.

These are what I have tried to pass along to you.

You may have read things here and there in these pages that left you with the offhand impression that, in bird-watching, appearances count for more than substance. Is this an attitude you should be especially concerned about? Not as long as you remember that when it comes to appearances, birding is much like life, and what counts is expensive brand names.

It is true that there are not many other pastimes where both the rank beginner and the true veteran are presented with so many opportunities to make themselves look like complete dopes, and so many different ways of doing it, but think of all the fresh air you get.

It has been people who are truly aware of their environments, who exist *in* their environments, who have kept humankind's progress from looking like a supermarket parking lot, asphalt stretching from beyond the horizon to beyond the horizon. It could be that *Down & Dirty Birding* has helped you become aware, or made you more aware if you were already aware, or made you extremely incredibly aware if you were already terrifically thoroughly aware. Or it could be that it has made you want to get into the paving business.

It is a chance you take with a book like this. Some things are better left unsaid.

Appendix:
The Basic Books

This book could not have been written without a great many other books. Here are some that I like a whole lot and have found extremely useful. They are also in human, rather than scientific, English.

The Audubon Society Encyclopedia of North American Birds, by John K. Terres (Alfred A. Knopf). Immense, magnificent, almost obsessively detailed. As close to everything between covers as it is possible to get.

The Cambridge Encyclopedia of Ornithology, edited by Michael Brooke and Tim Birkhead (Cambridge University Press). More global in scope, and a shade more technical, but perfectly readable.

The Birds of Canada, by W. Earl Godfrey (National Museums of Canada). Among definitive works, a definitive work.

The Birdwatchers Companion: An Encyclopedic Handbook of North American Birdlife, by Christopher Leahy (Hill and Wang). A shade less daunting than the *Audubon Encyclopedia*, and considerably more opinionated. A general reference with attitude.

Watching Birds: An Introduction to Ornithology, by Roger F. Pasquier (Houghton Mifflin). The one that got me hooked on reading about birds. The subject has never been more engaging. The Smithsonian Institution recommends the book to people taking its bird tours to bring them up to speed. It actually contains an illustration showing a rooster's feather tracts.

Hawks in Flight, by Pete Dunne, David Sibley, and Clay Sutton (Houghton Mifflin). For the real raptor junkie. Oy, gestalt!

The Beak of the Finch: A Story of Evolution in Our Time, by Jonathan Weiner (Knopf). All you need to know about what Darwin saw, what it means, and how evolution continues to work today.

Birds in Jeopardy: The Imperiled and Extinct Birds of the United States and Canada, by Paul R. Ehrlich, David S. Dobkin, and Darryl Wheye (Stanford University Press). The lowdown in a nutshell, plus some of Ehrlich's customarily pointed recommendations.

Introduced Birds of the World, by John L. Long (David & Charles). Among the charts and graphs, some hair-raising tales of how loony humankind can be.

Where the Birds Are: A Guide to All 50 States and Canada, by John Oliver Jones (Morrow). Bare-bones stuff. For the traveler in the United States, a good book to check before you head into unfamiliar territory. For the traveler in Canada, though, it is awfully thin.

Finding Birds Around the World, by Peter Alden and John Gooders (Houghton Mifflin). The same sort of thing but on a broader scale and with a whole lot more personality.

Roger Tory Peterson's Dozen Birding Hotspots, by George H. Harrison (Simon & Schuster). Harrison challenged Peterson to come up with a list of places, then visited them with an eye to the practicalities of footloose birding. Like many great bird books, it is out of print, but your library should have it.

The Travelling Birder: 20 Five-Star Birding Vacations, by Clive Goodwin (Doubleday). It provides a lovely sense of moving through the landscape, most of it in North America, but with expeditions to the Caribbean, Britain, Spain, and Kenya thrown in to make you thoroughly envious.

Goodwin is an industrious authority. He has done the two essential works on my home territory: *A Birdfinding Guide to the Toronto Region* (he and his wife published it themselves), and *A Birdfinding Guide to Ontario* (University of Toronto Press). If there is a nook or a cranny where birds lurk, it is in these books, with careful directions for finding it.

There are similar sorts of books for most localities on the continent and they are worth digging out before you start exploring. The most delightful are a series of birder's guides originated by James A. Lane for the American Birding Association, and thoughtfully revised since his death by Harold R. Holt. The cover slash still says "Lane's." They are folksy and even funny and can be mystically accurate, sometimes giving a street address where there is a specific bush guaranteed to contain a specific species. There are separate editions for Florida, southeastern

Arizona, Southern California, Colorado, the Rio Grande Valley, the Texas coast, and Churchill, Manitoba. For information:

The American Birding Association
P.O. Box 6599
Colorado Springs, CO 80934.

Index